Praying with Scripture

Reading with Scripture

Praying with Scripture

Maureen Gallagher
Clare Wagner, O.P.
David Woeste

Paulist Press
New York/Ramsey

Photo credits:

Orville Andrews: 4 (lower right)
Robert L. Beckhard: 92, 94
Jerry Bushey: 17
Ed Carlin: 112
Dwight Cendrowski: 104 (top)
Tom Cheek: 46, 62 (lower left), 63 (lower left)
Vivienne della Grotta: 4 (upper right), 50, 52, 62 (upper right), 63 (upper left, center right), 78, 96
Rohn Engh: 4 (upper left), 60, 62 (lower right), 74, 86, 95, 104 (bottom)
Kay Freeman: 63 (upper right)
Luke Golobitsh: 9, 16
Ed Lettau: 90
Mia et Klaus: 18 (bottom), 77, 80, 81
Paul M. Schrock: 32, 40, 42, 62 (upper left), 63 (lower right), 93
Vernon Sigl: 79
Rick Smolan: 4 (lower left), 63 (center)
David S. Strickler: 63 (center left)

Library of Congress
Catalog Card Number: 82-62923

ISBN: 0-8091-2544-7

Published by Paulist Press
545 Island Road, Ramsey, N.J. 07446

Printed and bound in the United States of America

Contents

Acknowledgements

Chapter 1
    "What Happens When We Die?" by Peter De Rosa in *PACE, Professional Approaches for Religious Educators,* Winona, Minnesota: St. Mary's College Press, 1974. Reprinted with permission.

Chapter 2
    Excerpt from *Markings* by Dag Hammarskjold, translated by Leif Sjoberg and W.H. Auden, New York: Alfred A. Knopf, Inc., 1965. Reprinted with permission.
    Excerpt from *Civilized Man's Eight Deadly Sins* by Konrad Lorenz, New York: Harcourt Brace Jovanovich, Inc., 1974. Reprinted with permission.
    "Prayer: You Can Come Home Again" by Ernest W. Ranly, C.P.P.S. with Ethel Gintoft, in *U.S. Catholic* (August 1975). Reprinted with permission.
    Excerpt from *The Little Prince* by Antoine de Saint-Exupéry, New York: Harcourt Brace Jovanovich, Inc., 1971. Reprinted with permission.
    Excerpt from *The Divine Milieu* by Pierre Teilhard de Chardin, New York: Harper and Row, 1960. Reprinted with permission.
    Excerpt from *Prayer, Living with God* by Simon Tugwell. Springfield, Illinois: Templegate Publishers, 1976. Reprinted with permission.

Chapter 4
    Excerpts from *The Honorary Consul* by Graham Greene, New York: Simon and Schuster, 1973. Reprinted with permission.
    Excerpts from *Loose in the World* by Thomas F. O'Meara, O.P. New York: Paulist Press, 1974. Reprinted with permission.

Chapter 5
    Excerpts from *Fullness of Life,* copyright © Concacan Inc. 1978. Reproduced with permission of the Canadian Conference of Catholic Bishops, 90 Parent Ave., Ottawa, Ontario K1N 7B1.

Chapter 7
    Excerpts from *Documents of Vatican II,* "Dogmatic Constitution on the Church." Copyright © 1966. New York: America Press, 1966. Reprinted with permission.

Chapter 8
    Excerpts from "Saint Joan" by Bernard Shaw in *Collected Plays.* London: Dodd Mead, 1970. Reprinted with permission of the Society of Authors, London, England, on behalf of the Bernard Shaw Estate.
    Excerpts from *Journeys,* ed. by Gregory Baum. New York: Paulist Press, 1975. Reprinted with permission.

Chapter 9
    "The Lord's Prayer" from *Bread for the Wilderness, Wine for the Journey* by John Killinger. Waco, Texas: Word Books, 1976. Reprinted with permission.
    Excerpts from "Catechetics in a Future Tense" by John Nelson in *New Catholic World* (January–February 1972). Reprinted with permission.

Chapter 10
    Excerpts from "Waiting for Insight" by John S. Dunne in *Prayer, Ritual and the Spiritual Life,* "Supplementary Series Number 5" (June 1975). Published by the *Anglican Theological Review.* Reprinted with permission.

    All Scripture quotations are taken from *The Jerusalem Bible,* copyright © 1966 by Darton, Longman & Todd, Ltd. and Doubleday & Company, Inc. Reprinted by permission of the publisher. All rights reserved.

Introduction

This is a book about developing prayer life and deepening a relationship with God and the Christian community. As Christians we look to religion for meaning in our lives and are taught that personal prayer is a way to find and deepen that meaning. *Praying with Scripture* presents ideas for a scripturally oriented understanding of prayer and suggests some practical ways of praying.

Regardless of your age, sex or occupation, you may be well aware of the need to pray yet not know how to meet the challenge of developing a prayer life. *Praying with Scripture* is a prayer-process book which enables you to study the source of the felt call to prayer and examine various ways of praying. It's designed to help people pray.

The Judaeo-Christian tradition includes a rich tradition of prayer, from the deeply personal and poetic expressions found in the psalms to the Our Father, which Jesus taught his disciples. The saints have sometimes left a record of their unique relationships with God. St. John of the Cross and St. Teresa of Avila are among those whose works have become part of our rich living heritage. All of this affirms that we are each called to relate deeply to God and to one another.

Importance of Prayer

Prayer is essential for the mature faith-life we seek as Christians. Yet there are real difficulties in developing a prayer life and experiencing meaningful prayer. *Praying with Scripture* addresses the challenge of communicating with God, which is the essence of prayer. What does God want to say to us? What do we want to say to God? How does this process of communication happen? How does our relationship with God develop?

God speaks to us through Scripture, creation, people, events, solitude, community and service. He longs for our response. We respond when we listen in solitude, or with others, when we speak our word from the depths of our hearts and then when we move out to share the good news we have heard. The process of becoming aware of God's presence and his ways, of being touched and changed by that presence and of sharing the good news is what we mean by prayer life. In this book we encourage the use of your Bible and writing a journal as ways of understanding the fuller meaning of "God with us."

Use of This Book by an Individual

A process for praying is integrated into this book. Thus we suggest that you "do" rather than "read." One learns to pray by *praying*, not by reading about it. We've included questions and photos to stimulate creative reflection and thought. You'll find that each chapter includes enough prayer material for about two to three hours. We encourage each of you to discover your own prayer rhythm and use the material accordingly. It may well be that you'll have only twenty to thirty minutes to spend in serious reflection at any given time.

Setting

As much as possible, begin by creating an environment which is conducive to quiet moments and prayer. Pictures, photos, music and flowers can be helpful. Glance through the chapter being used to get a feel for its themes and activities. Rearrange furniture, pick some flowers or choose music that will enhance the theme of the chapter. This preparation is neither silly nor trivial. It's like setting the table for company. Candlelight, music, flowers, a locked door for privacy—all can greatly enhance your prayer experience.

It's certainly possible to pray without changing your environment. One homemaker can spare only two five-minute periods away from her small children. She uses these periods to begin her prayer and then continues praying while she cooks, folds laundry and does her other routine household tasks. Similarly, an office worker uses her time commuting by bus for prayer and reflection. Prayer depends not on ideal circumstances but on the desire and imagination of a person who seriously wants to get in touch with his or her inner life.

Use of This Book by a Group

Praying with Scripture is designed to be adaptable to many situations. A parish might want to use it with those in a catechumenal formation program, for groups being confirmed, for those preparing for marriage and even for prayer programs during liturgical seasons such as Christmas and Easter. The activities lend themselves to community building.

You may also decide to form a home prayer group with neighbors, family or friends. You'll find that the courage and initiative needed to form a group will be well repaid as you share prayer experiences and discern common prayer concerns and goals.

The suggestions given above about the setting and environment are especially important for group prayer. We strongly recommend using candles, music or other things in the environment which will enhance the themes of the chapter being used.

If your prayer group, whether at home or in a parish, is larger than five or six people, you'll want to refer to the companion volume to this handbook entitled the *Praying with Scripture Manual*.

Frequency of Prayer Sessions

Any attempt to accomplish as much as possible as *quickly* as possible will defeat the purpose of this book. Sufficient time is needed between sessions to "practice" and to let the experience become a part of your life and of you.

We recommend that group sessions be held once a week for an hour or two. It is important to use some of the prayer activities between sessions. The final activities in each chapter are designed to be used privately between sessions to promote and sustain personal prayer.

Bible and Notebook

Many of the Scripture quotations in *Praying with Scripture* are referenced rather than quoted. Thus it's important for you to have a Bible to use as you read the chapters. We also strongly recommend that you have a notebook that can be used as a journal. Chapter 3, "Journal Writing: A Help in Praying," initiates you into keeping a journal, and subsequent chapters suggest times and reflections for journal keeping.

Some Suggestions Before Beginning

1. Whether using *Praying with Scripture* alone or in a group we recommend looking over the whole chapter *before* you use it for meditation. It's very helpful to know the theme and to prepare an appropriate setting for prayer. This is especially important for a group.

2. In a prayer group rotate the responsibility for leading the sessions. Each participant should have a copy of this handbook so that he or she can make appropriate preparations for the group sessions and carry out the prayer activities.

3. When using the book alone or with a small group try reading the passages aloud. A slow, meditative reading of the passages is important. For a group you might even have a lector, teacher, or parish priest record the readings on a cassette before the session.

Sexist Language

The authors have made a decision not to change sexist language in articles from which they quote; they also did not change it in biblical quotations in deference to the original language choice of the authors. There has been a concerted effort to avoid sexist language in the remainder of the text.

Chapter 1

The Call to Prayer

A Quest for Prayer: Who am I? Who is God?

As we begin to discover the richness of a life of prayer, we should consider the image we have of ourselves and the image we have of God. Throughout history, people have searched for ways to describe themselves and their God. The Scriptures are full of such descriptions. As they are used in Scripture, the images are dynamic and ever-changing. They reflect the growth of people in their relationships with one another and with God; they describe the understanding people have about life and death.

All of Life is a Vocation to Prayer

The human personality has different "facets" or "dimensions." One psychiatrist has said that there are basically four different "persons" in each of us: (1) the person I think I am; (2) the person you think I am; (3) the person I really am; (4) the person I can become. One of the reasons we pray is to become better acquainted with these different facets of our personalities.

The English word *enthusiasm* derives from the Greek words *en theos,* meaning "in God." When I fully and honestly know all the facets of my being—my space in God—then I can be enthusiastic about life and more fully and accurately respond to my destiny—my calling in life. That is why prayer demands that we take a long and loving look at ourselves and our relationship to others. Through a better understanding, acceptance and realization of the complex gift of life and calling to life that is in us, we make "space" in ourselves for God.

Every one of us has a vocation to prayer. It surfaces from the very complexity of our being, and even from our imperfections. We learn from the story of Adam and Eve that they discovered they were imperfect lovers. As a result, they realized the need to reorientate themselves to their Creator—to make room, or space, "in God." One important aspect of prayer is the need to renew continually our orientation to the God who has given us life in abundance.

For Reflection

1. Enumerate the four different "persons" in you. Does this make sense to you? Can you see these four dimensions in your life? What are the different "sides" of your personality that show themselves?
2. What is the origin of the word *enthusiasm?* Does knowing the origin of the word give you any new insights into its meaning?
3. Why is prayer important to you? Is it an activity outside yourself? Or is it much more personal? How would you speak of prayer to another person?
4. Read Deuteronomy 30:15–20. What does this passage mean for you? How does it relate to the topic of prayer?

Images of God

We think of prayer in terms of relating to God. In any relationship, we want to know what kind of person we are speaking to and listening to. To what images of God do we relate? Inadequate images of God have come to us from the past because of undeveloped understandings or distortions passed on through the ages. Do any of the following images seem familiar? Some people have thought of God as cruel, one who wants us to suffer, who inflicts suffering on us. In fact, they see suffering as a sign of love. Others have thought of the deity as a testing God, one who deliberately puts us through difficult times simply to see whether we can make it. Still others have thought of God as an avenging judge who watches over us, scrutinizes our actions, evaluates us, and has all kinds of plans to punish us. A more mature image of God is an image of a loving and challenging God; a God who is touched by who we are and what we do. This image is well reflected in a passage found in Isaiah 43:1–4:

> Do not be afraid, for I have redeemed you;
> I have called you by name, you are mine.
> Should you pass through the sea, I will be with you;
> or through rivers, they shall not swallow you up.
> Should you walk through fire, you shall not be scorched
> and the flames will not burn you.
> For I am Yahweh your God,
> the Holy One, your Savior. . . .

6

Because you are precious in my eyes,
because you are honored and I love you,
I give men in exchange for you,
peoples in return for your life.
Do not be afraid for I am with you.

For Reflection

After reading the above paragraph on Images of God, use the diagram to write your ideas or to sketch symbols that express your past and present image of God.

Images of God Diagram

Images of God that have been suggested or taught to me.

Images of God as I have come to
know him through my experience and
searching.

Images of God as I would like him to
be.

Use this space to jot down feelings,
ideas, understandings, or questions
that come from reflection on what you
have put in the top three spaces.

Reflection:
Getting in Touch with Your
Personal Relationship with God
Isaiah 43:1–4

But now, thus says Yahweh,
who created you, Jacob,
who formed you, Israel:
Do not be afraid, for I have redeemed you;
I have called you by your name, you are mine.
Should you pass through the sea, I will be with you;
or through rivers, they will not swallow you up.
Should you walk through fire, you will not be scorched
and the flames will not burn you.
For I am Yahweh, your God,
the Holy One of Israel, your Savior.
I give Egypt for your ransom,
and exchange Cush and Seba for you.
Because you are precious in my eyes,
because you are honored and I love you,
I give men in exchange for you,
peoples in return for your life.

1. As you read this passage, put your own name in the place of Israel and Jacob. Be very quiet and notice how it feels to have God saying these things directly to you. Can you recall fears, "seas" or "fires" you have experienced recently? Think of these; share them with your God who is with you.

2. In your own words, ask God to help you believe that you are precious in his eyes and that he is with you.

Hosea 11:1–4

> When Israel was a child I loved him,
> and I called my son out of Egypt.
> But the more I called to them, the further they went from me;
> they have offered sacrifice to the Baals
> and set their offerings smoking before the idols.
> I myself taught Ephraim to walk,
> I took them in my arms;
> yet they have not understood that I was the one looking after them.
> I led them with reins of kindness,
> with leading-strings of love.
> I was like someone who lifts an infant close against his cheek;
> stooping down to him I give him his food.

1. As you read, notice the words and phrases that show the tenderness of God's love. Have you ever thought of or experienced God as someone who is tender toward you? Recall that time. Thank him for it.

2. Recall a time when you went far from God. Remember that time; share it in prayer with God.

3. "I led them with reins of kindness, with leading-strings of love." What have been the "reins of kindness," the "leading-strings of love" that have led you to deeper faith? Who was involved? Where did these events take place? Recall them and thank God for them.

Jeremiah 1:4–10

The word of Yahweh was addressed to me, saying,

> "Before I formed you in the womb I knew you;
> before you came to birth I consecrated you;
> I have appointed you as prophet to the nations."

I said, "Ah, Lord Yahweh; look, I do not know how to speak: I am a child!" But Yahweh replied,

> "Do not say, 'I am a child.'
> Go now to those to whom I send you
> and say whatever I command you.
> Do not be afraid of them,
> for I am with you to protect you—
> it is Yahweh who speaks!"

10

Then Yahweh put out his hand and touched my mouth and said to me:

> "There! I am putting my words in your mouth.
> Look, today I am setting you
> over nations and over kingdoms,
> to tear up and to knock down,
> to destroy and to overthrow,
> to build and to plant."

1. Recall an incident in which you felt as weak as a child, but in which you received strength from somewhere to do what you had to do.
2. With this incident in mind, read the above passage and put yourself in Jeremiah's shoes, listening to the words as if they were spoken to you.

All of life is a call to prayer. This article is about the moment of death, perhaps the most important moment in life.

What Happens When We Die?
by Peter DeRosa

I remember, when I was a student in Rome fifteen years ago, being invited to tea by an elderly American lady married to an Italian prince. In her quiet, Passolini-coloured villa outside the City, we talked together for a couple of hours about religion. She told me how, as a young woman, she had read the classical two-volume work, *Marius The Epicurean*. It had given her, she said, a lasting voluptuous appreciation of the joys of life.

"And afterwards, Principessa?"

"Ah," she replied, as if peering into the dark, "who knows?"

And she quoted a poem about mysticism called "The Moth." Three days later she sent me a copy of the relevant lines in her large, clear handwriting.

> The Moth
> Who folded his wings within and so became
>
> One colour and one substance with the flame.
> He only knew the flame who in it burned.
> And only he could tell, who ne'er to tell returned.

Yet do we not all have what Berdyaev calls "moments of communion with eternity"? T.S. Eliot, while claiming that to apprehend the point of intersection of the timeless with time is an occupation for the saint, still says:

> For most of us, there is only the unattended
> Moment, the moment in and out of time,
> The distraction fit, lost in a shaft of sunlight,
> The wild thyme unseen, or the winter lightning

11

> Or the waterfall, or music heard so deeply
> That it is not heard at all, but you are the music
> While the music lasts.

We all have these "hints and guesses" at eternity. It may be the experience of falling in love and grasping that a basic and tragic estrangement has been banished for ever; or the birth of one's child, proving that love is endless; or the simple sense of the grandeur that anything at all should exist. ("Why should there be something and not nothing?—that is the profoundest question of philosophy.")

If I had to choose one phrase to cover these experiences, I would prefer to speak of "a sense of oneness or kinship with all that is." We begin and end physically one with the universe, even with the dust. And our spiritual task is to recognize and to accept a oneness on a higher plane, and by acceptance to create it.

Take the case of the North American Indians: when they die, they like to think they are feeding the generous earth that fed them. Or the Bushmen of the Kalihari desert who are buried facing the rising sun and who breathe their last into the great Wind of which they always were a part. In this line of thought, St. Paul pictures the broad, loved earth as a Mother writhing in the pangs of birth: "We know that the whole creation has been groaning in travail together until now" (Rom. 8:22).

The sense of oneness or kinship I am trying to describe is most intense at the personal level. We feel in such moments that all human beings—who ever were or are or are to be—are one with us, one family with us; they *are* us. In this perspective, time is overturned; it does not matter. As the Zen poet puts it:

> And all those happenings a billion years ago
> Are happening around us now, all around us: time.
> Indeed this morning the sparrow hopped about
> In that nebulous whirlpool
> A million light years hence.

Thomas Merton, in his essay, *The Zen Revival,* says we need the recognition "that the whole world is aware of itself in me, and that 'I' am no longer limited to my individual and empirical self, still less to a disembodied soul, but that my 'identity' is to be sought not in that *separation* from all that is, but in *oneness* with all that is. This identity is not the denial of my own personal reality but its highest affirmation."

The experience of birth certainly points to oneness and communion, but so does death, without which birth in our kind of world is impossible.

Saint-Exupéry, who died in an aircrash—presumably he was shot down by the Nazis—depicts this brilliantly in his *Flight To Arras.* When about to go on a wartime sortie, he used to imagine the flesh reeling under the impending blows from enemy shells. He felt so vulnerable. But the body—what is it, this domesticated animal he had taken all those years to the tailor, the doctor, the barber? In the moment of trial, when a man's little boy is in danger in a burning house or the battle flares up, he discovers the body is only a rag, an encumbrance, easily parted with. "It is in your act that you exist, not in your body."

12

Then he realizes: "If he should die, he would not be cutting himself off from his kind, but making himself one with them. He would not be losing himself, but finding himself."

And the final illumination: "There is no death when you meet death. When the body sinks into death, the essence of man is revealed. Man is a knot, a web, a mesh into which relationships are tied. Only those relationships matter. The body is an old crock that nobody will miss. I have never known a man to think of himself when dying. Never."

All that I have written so far is familiar territory to the reader of the Bible. From beginning to end, it is a story of kinship and brotherhood. It really is there on the very first page.

If only we had realized earlier that Adam means Mankind and Eve means Life. The Genesis myth teaches that each person contains within himself the whole of mankind and the life of the world. All men are responsible for each man, and each man is responsible for all. There is also original sin; it is not the race inheriting the sin of the individual but the individual inheriting the sin of the race. This, too, is the consequence of man's solidarity with all his brethren.

Christ comes to bring this oneness to a higher level in the Kingdom of God. He vitalizes the life of the world with his own life of communion with the Father-God. But the question, "How does Christ influence all men?" is particularly fruitless in the light of Biblical teaching. For the Bible tells us from the start that everything anyone does *must* affect everyone else. In this instance as well, Christ is not the grand exception but the supreme example of the rule. John was right to put on Jesus' lips: "Unless the grain of wheat falling into the ground dies, it remains alone. But if it dies, it brings forth much fruit." Christ was supremely Representative Man who found in death there was no death but only a deeper communion with his kind.

Christianity is brotherhood in Christ. And for the purpose of these articles I want to stress this aspect of the mystery of Christ: He is still among us, suffering and rejoicing, living and dying.

When Paul hears Christ say, "Saul, Saul, why are you persecuting me?" or Pascal writes, "Jesus will be in agony till the end of the world," we cluck with admiration and confess it to be profound theology—and promptly forget about it. We go on imagining Christ in his heaven a billion miles away; we project the blessed who have "passed on" as dwelling in a paradise from which all acquaintance with evil has been excluded by a benign providence.

The truth is that, by dying, Christ has "passed over" to his Father, hence he is one with us in his Spirit. He is nearer than he ever was. He is "the knot, the web, the mesh into which all human relationships are tied." And, once again, what is true of Christ is true of us. When we die, the world becomes more really our body. In it, in our fellow human beings, our brothers and sisters, we suffer and rejoice, we live and we die.

You may know the ancient Zen story of a warrior approaching a Zen master to enquire if there is a heaven and a hell. The master taunts the Samurai about his unwarlike and beggarly looks. At this, the Samurai begins to draw his sword. More goading from the master about its dullness and bluntness. And now the sword is fully drawn. "Here," said the master, "open the gates of hell." The warrior sheathed his sword. "Here," the master said, "open the gates of paradise."

No, hell isn't a matter of revenge. It is a plain fact. It is in our acts that we exist; we are what we have chosen to be. We can choose by forsaking God to become God-forsaken people.

What I want to add to this is first the realization that the world is our body, the world of human relationships, of love and mercy, hatred and tenderness. What we have chosen to be is what the world has become through us because *we* are the knot, the web, the mesh of the world. Hell is not in another world into which the departing soul is plunged; nor is hell simply within the soul. Hell's gates open wide onto the world we are in the process of making. And heaven, too. The whole of mankind that has "passed over" as Christ has is suffering in the world's hell and rejoicing in its paradise.

The second truth I want to add to the traditional depiction of life after death is the communion of . . . sinners. All of us are sinners. All have fallen short of the glory of God. All of us to some degree have harboured hell within us and live in hell. If I'm right in thinking of life after death as essentially participation in the ongoing life of *this* world and not of some distant other-world, then we must repudiate the idea of a kind of isolated existence whether in a remote heaven or even a more remote hell.

When I die, I do not want to go away from this world, unless, like Christ, I come in the Spirit closer to it, sharing more keenly in all its hopes and concerns. In a real sense, I do not care a fig for what happens anywhere except in this world, for I do not really believe in "anywhere else." Like Christ, I do not think I am here to save my soul; I am here to join him in saving the world. Nietzsche said a very profound thing; we mustn't on any account shift the center of gravity of life *out of* life into some Beyond, into Nothingness.

I believe that death gives us a deeper entry into fellowship. Perhaps we can speak of it no more lucidly than the singed moth can speak of the flame. But it is my conviction, based on "a moment in and out of time," that even the lost are not entirely lost, even though they be eternally lost. Eternally lost, in the sense that their contribution which *might* have been made will *never* be made. But not entirely lost because in that newfound fellowship, the blessed in us suffers from the pangs of hell, and the damned in us rejoices in the good that all the saints and all sinners have done.

For Reflection

1. How does this author try to give us some "hints and guesses" or concrete examples of what eternity is like? Do you have any similar experiences or insights to share?

2. What does the author mean by "a sense of oneness or kinship with all that is"? How does this relate to our consideration of prayer?

3. Saint-Exupéry uses a good example of sacrifice, relating it to the meaning of our existence. What is the example he uses? What image did Jesus use in a similar way? How does his death relate to our living today?

Bibliography

Egan, Keith. *What Is Prayer?* Denville: Dimension Books, 1973.

Frankl, Viktor E. *Man's Search for Meaning.* New York: Pocket Books, 1963.

Fynn, *Mister God, This Is Anna.* New York: Holt, Rinehart & Winston, 1974.

Guillet, Jacques. *A God Who Speaks.* New York: Paulist Press, 1977.

Guthrie, Woody. *Bound for Glory.* New York: Dutton, 1968.

Hammarskjold, Dag. *Markings.* New York: Alfred A. Knopf, 1965.

Hesse, Hermann. *Siddhartha.* New York: Bantam Books, 1951.

Lang, Martin. *Acquiring Our Image of God.* New York: Paulist Press, 1983.

McNeill, Donald, Morrison, Douglas, Nouwen, Henri. *Compassion.* New York: Doubleday, 1982.

Raines, Robert. *To Kiss the Joy.* Waco: Word Books, 1973.

Article

Senior, Donald. "Teach Us To Pray," *New Catholic World,* March/April 1983.

Chapter 2

Invitation to Meditation

1. "Whoever drinks this water
   will get thirsty again;
   but anyone who drinks the water that I shall give will never be thirsty again:
   the water that I shall give will turn into a spring inside him, welling up to eternal life."

   (John 4:14)

2. "I stand on the shores of the deep.
   I play at the ocean's edge.
   The waters splash upon the shore;
   animals and children celebrate the sound,
   the coolness of the water,
   of the water's dance upon the shore."
   (Anonymous)

3. "He turned a desert into sheets of water,
and an arid country into flowing springs,
where he gave the hungry a home
in which to found a habitable town." (*Psalm 107:35–36*)

4. "Save me, God; the water
is already up to my neck!
I am sinking in the deepest swamp,
there is no foothold;
I have stepped into deep water
and the waves are washing over me." (*Psalm 69:1–2*)

18

5. "Let the sea thunder and all that it holds,
   and the world, with all who live in it;
   let all the rivers clap their hands
   and the mountains shout for joy." (*Psalm 98:7–8*)

Meditation: An Active Response to Life

Meditation is a process of reflecting on one's life and one's relationship to God and others. It is an essential ingredient in a life of prayer. Meditation is not merely a passive exercise; rather it is an active response to life with its joys and pains, anxieties and struggles. It is an active response to the presence of God-in-life. Meditation involves quieting oneself, listening to the inner movements of one's life, one's relationship to God, and to others, and responding to the inner beckonings of the heart and mind in prayer.

To meditate one must be able to imagine, to wonder, to be open to mystery, and to feel deeply the experience of the moment. Meditation requires a type of childlikeness, an openness to the non-material world, and the ability to quiet oneself in order to get in touch with the inner workings of one's existence.

Matthew's Meditation

It might seem strange to think that a child's attempt at meditation could help adults to pray, but I would like to share some insights I received from a young boy named Matthew. He is an ordinary eleven-year-old boy who believes in God, loves football, fights with his brothers, is punished by his parents, dreams about his future, and has a very good imagination. When he was asked how he would teach someone to meditate, he said:

> "I'd say, just close your eyes and think about things you did in the past and things that you think are going to happen. Think about all the things you like or the sad things that happen in life."

When Matthew meditates, he sometimes thinks about sad things. He lets himself experience the feelings connected with them and then he "gets them off his chest," as he says. In our reflection, we also need to recognize sad or unpleasant experiences and feelings; we need to acknowledge them and work them through.

But Matthew thinks about the happy things in his life, too; he says that remembering them makes him happier still. Remembering moments of joy, growth, love and celebration strengthens and affirms him and encourages him to go on. As Matthew says: "Another happy thing is if you make a really good touchdown in football. You are happy and everyone is jumping on you, saying, 'Great touchdown!' "

Matthew sees God as the one who makes possible his meditation, his feelings, his experiences, his life. When he was asked why he thought God created him, Matthew replied, " 'Cause he wanted someone to love, and to help, and he didn't want to be alone always."

Matthew's comments on meditation contain some good suggestions for our own prayer. To reflect on our own experiences, to come to see where God fits into the picture of our lives, and to take time for solitude are the first steps in everyone's spiritual journey.

For Reflection
1. Do Matthew's comments bring to mind things you have heard children say about prayer or about God?
2. Can you remember times of solitude, insight, and closeness to God from your own childhood? Reflect on them.
3. What are some points that Matthew makes about meditation which you think apply to adult meditations? What insights did you get from Matthew for your own practice of meditation?

A Meditation About Water

A person who meditates is one who imagines, who wonders, who sees with eyes open to mystery, who feels deeply the experience of the moment. A person who meditates is one who can look at water and let it speak of peace and power, of turbulence and challenge.

Use the pictures of water at the beginning of this chapter and their accompanying quotations to initiate meditation. The following questions for reflection may help to structure your meditation.

1. Water can be calm, can cleanse, can destroy. Recall times in your life when water calmed you, cleansed you, endangered you.
2. Why did Jesus use water as an image? Reflect on the words from John, "Whoever drinks this water will get thirsty again; but anyone who drinks the water that I shall give will never be thirsty again: the water that I shall give will turn into a spring inside him, welling up to eternal life" (John 4:14). What is the water Jesus will give?
3. When have you found yourself in "deep waters?" When has this depth been a positive experience? When has it been a negative experience?

What Is Meditation?

Directions. Write true or false before each of the following statements. Take your time; reflect on each statement. After you have finished, turn to the following pages and check your answers. Read the explanations slowly and carefully.

_____ 1. The approach to meditation is the same in Eastern and Western religions.
_____ 2. Reflecting on water or fire can be a meditation.
_____ 3. The aim of meditation is to meet God and develop a relationship with him.
_____ 4. The imagination plays a significant role in meditation.
_____ 5. Meditation is not ordinary prayer; it is for those with special gifts and a lot of time for prayer.
_____ 6. All people do not need time for themselves or for solitude. Solitude is only for individuals with a special call.
_____ 7. The Spirit is working in the life of every person.
_____ 8. Some preparation is necessary for our meeting with God and an awareness of his presence.
_____ 9. It is possible to say prayers and attend church services and not experience God.
_____ 10. There is an inner, non-material world as well as an outer, material world, and we all have access to that inner world.
_____ 11. Only good feelings of joy, thanksgiving, happiness, and hope are experienced in meditation.
_____ 12. Our American lifestyle provides a good environment for meditative prayer and spiritual growth.

1. **False.** Eastern ways of meditating differ from those in the West. Eastern religions usually stress discipline, detachment, the loss of personhood, and becoming one with pure consciousness. Western Christians stress response to God's loving concern expressed in Jesus. Both approaches can offer much to each other; aspects of Eastern meditation complement and enrich Western styles of prayer.

2. **True.** Reflecting on water can easily be a meditation because it has a quieting effect, can stimulate a response to images, helps one's appreciation of God's creation, and thereby prepares our hearts, minds, and spirits to experience God.

3. **True.** The goal of meditation is to establish a relationship with God. Meditation can also lead to self-knowledge and a better relationship with others and the world.

4. **True.** Imagination, intuition, and wonderment are needed in order to find God's presence in our experience. Imagination expands the horizons for understanding our experience.

5. **False.** Meditation is our preparation for experiencing God; it is ordinary and for every believer. Perhaps limited numbers of people are called to mystical prayer, but everyone has a vocation to establish a relationship with God. Few artists are as famous as Michelangelo, but everyone has some artistic talents such as cooking, gardening, sewing, and building. So, too, *some* people are famous for their skills at prayer, but *all* are called to pray.

6. **False.** Solitude, reflective time alone, is a basic human need. It can be as little as fifteen minutes a day or one day a month, but it is necessary for anyone who wishes to live a truly human life.

7. **True.** "The Spirit of God fills the whole earth" and works in each person. We can ignore or reject the Spirit. These sessions are designed to help us become more conscious of the Spirit in us and to open ourselves more completely to him.

8. **True.** To learn to see with the eyes of faith and hear with the ears of faith is the goal of Christian life. Meditation helps us to silence ourselves so that we can hear God speak. It helps us open our eyes to see his power in the ocean, his beauty in the flower, his majesty in the mountains.

9. **True.** Just mouthing words or making gestures is never enough. We need to encounter the mystery and the person of God. Our church services, the liturgy, will only be as good as the depth of prayer that individuals bring with them. The liturgy is like a mighty ocean into which many individuals pour living streams of personal prayer.

10. **True.** Our dreams and our intuitions are proof of the inner life and activity in each of us. Meditation helps us to get comfortable in that inner world and to find God present there.

11. **False.** In meditation we often uncover our angers, frustrations, pains, and struggles. We can also bring these to God. God is with us in all the feelings and experiences of life, not just the positive ones.

12. **False.** The American culture and lifestyle frequently undervalues silence, solitude, simplicity, and the inner world. Americans have to combat the influence of many aspects of their culture to become people of serious prayer, but it is possible.

Thoughts on Solitude and Meaning in Life

Use these quotations for reflection during a time of quiet.

1. From *Prayer, Living With God,* by Simon Tugwell
    (a) "Modern man has forgotten what talking means. We talk so much that we have lost the ability to distinguish between talking when we have got something to say, and just talking for the sake of talking. We have found it increasingly difficult just to sit quietly with some-one—we would really prefer to have everyone talking at once. If we were less afraid of silence, we might discover once again how to say things when we have got something to say, and so discover the meaningfulness of conversation."

When have I been really silent lately? When did I have the last conversation I would call "meaningful?"

    (b) "To say to God 'give me humility,' when I do not want humility is self-defeating. Maybe I know that I ought to want humility; but in that case I should say, 'I do not really want humility, but I know I ought to. Please make me want it.' If we are too shy to say anything at all to God, then perhaps we should just sit quietly for a while and not try to say anything. On the other hand, we may be overcome with confusion and say whatever comes into our head first. All these are ordinary human uses of language. And we are human beings, and it is our humanity that is redeemed in Jesus Christ. So let us not be afraid to use human language in human ways when we draw close to God."

What words would I use to speak my feelings to God right now?

2. From *The Little Prince* by Antoine de Saint-Exupéry
    "My life is very monotonous," (the fox) said. "I hunt chickens; men hunt me. All the chickens are just alike, and all the men are just alike. And, in consequence, I am a little bored. But if you tame me, it will be as if the sun came to shine on my life. I shall know the sound of a step that will be different from all the others. Other steps send me hurrying back underneath the ground. Yours will call me, like music, out of my burrow." "What must I do to tame you?" asked the little prince. "You must be very patient," replied the fox. "First you will sit down at a little distance from me—like that—in the grass. I shall look at you out of the corner of my eye, and you will say nothing. Words are the source of misunderstandings. But you will sit a little closer to me, every day. . . ." "Goodbye," said the fox. "And now here is my secret, a very simple secret: It is only with the heart that one can see rightly; what is essential is invisible to the eye."

Recall the name of a person who has "tamed" you; a person you have "tamed." Remember and give thanks.

3. From *Civilized Man's Eight Deadly Sins* by Konrad Lorenz

   "One of the worst effects of haste, or of the fear engendered by it, is the apparent inability of modern man to spend even the shortest time alone. He anxiously avoids every possibility of self-communion or meditation, as though he feared that reflection might present him with a ghastly self-portrait, such as that of Dorian Gray. The only explanation for the widespread addiction to noise is that something has to be suppressed. One day, when my wife and I were walking in the woods, we were surprised to hear the rapidly approaching metallic sounds of a transistor radio. As its owner, a lone, sixteen-year-old cyclist came into view, my wife remarked, 'He's afraid of hearing the birds sing.' I think he was only afraid of meeting himself. Why, otherwise, do perfectly intelligent people prefer the inane advertisements on television to their own company? I am sure it is because it helps them to dispel reflection."

How can I be free from noise occasionally? What noise bothers me? Do I like to reflect? Why?

4. From *The Divine Milieu* by Teilhard de Chardin

   "And so for the first time in my life perhaps (although I am supposed to meditate every day) I took the lamp, and leaving the zone of everyday occupations and relationships where everything seems clear, I went down into my inmost self, to the deep abyss whence I felt dimly that my power of action emanates. But as I moved further and further away from the conventional certainties by which social life is superficially illuminated, I became more aware of the descent, a new person was disclosed within me, of whose name I am no longer sure, and who no longer obeyed me. And when I had to stop my exploration because the path faded beneath my steps, I found a bottomless abyss at my feet, and out of it came— arising I knew not from where—the current which I dared to call my life."

Have I dared to journey to my "inmost self"? What have I found there?

5. From *Markings* by Dag Hammerskjold

   "I don't know who—or what—put the question, I don't know when it was put. I don't even remember answering. But at the moment I did answer Yes to Someone—or Something— and from that hour I was certain that existence is meaningful and that, therefore, my life in self-surrender, had a goal. From that moment I have known what it means 'not to look back,' and 'to take no thought for the morrow.' "

Have I given a significant Yes in my life? To whom? What meaning and goal is clear in my life?

6. Statement made by Pablo Picasso, source unknown

   "Nothing can be done without solitude. I have made a solitude for myself which no one has ever imagined. It is very hard to be alone nowadays. We've got watches. Have you ever seen a saint with a watch? I've looked everywhere to try to find one, even among the saints considered to be the watchmakers' patrons."

Does solitude have a place in my life? How do I feel about being alone and quiet?

7. From a retreat at the Cenacle in Chicago, Illinois

"As we become quiet the energies that we have spent in moving about our daily lives can move inward. We become more free to work and to become aware of our deepest self, our deepest desires, hopes and dreams. The more we are able to listen to these and to accept their presence, the more closely we can begin to listen to that quieter call from God in the midst of them. In this deepening stillness—without and within—we will be taught by God; we will develop new eyes and ears and will learn new things."

Can I name one deep desire, hope, dream that I have? How are these connected to God in my life?

Reflections

Reflect on the following passages from Scripture when you can set aside twenty or thirty minutes for meditation.

1. Sit in a quiet, comfortable place. Light a candle, if you wish, or play some meditative background music. Give your concerns to the Lord, breathe deeply, allow yourself to become very quiet, and simply sit for a few minutes.
2. Read the Scripture passage slowly and let the words touch you.
3. Use the questions, if you wish, to help you reflect on the passage.
4. Close your prayer by speaking your feelings to God in your own words.

I. The Parable of the Mustard Seed, Mark 4:30–32
1. Imagine a mustard seed, its size, its potential. Picture such a seed being planted and growing.
2. How has the kingdom of God, your faith, been planted in you? How has it grown over the years? What experiences have watered it and helped it to grow? What experiences have been difficult ones, or ones providing very little growth?

II. The Parable of the Pearl, Matthew 13:45–46
1. Imagine a pearl, what it looks like, how it feels. If you know Steinbeck's story *The Pearl,* recall how precious the pearl was and the problems that occurred because of its use.
2. Are there any things or persons that are pearls of great price in your life? What have they "cost" you in pain, time, care, love, and so on? If you had to sell everything to buy the pearl described in Scripture, what would you sell first? What would you sell last?
3. Do you feel that God, your faith, and the kingdom are precious to you? What do you do to "keep" those precious gifts?

III. The Parable of the Sower, Matthew 13:24–30

1. After you have read the story, sit back and picture the whole thing happening. Imagine yourself standing on a road very close to the field and watching the action. Notice the color, size, and shape of the field; the age and appearance of the sower and the owner.

2. What do you consider as the wheat growing in the field of your life, and what do you consider as the weeds growing with the wheat? What are your feelings about your "wheat" and your "weeds"?

Prayer: You Can Come Home Again
by Father Ernest W. Ranly, C.PP.S. with Ethel Gintoft

When my father died, over a dozen years ago, the funeral services were all in Latin, with black vestments and with the praying of many rosaries. The little parish church in German-Catholic Mercer County, Ohio, has the traditional cemetery nearby; the large crowd followed the bier to the cemetery for a very proper interment. A priest-friend told me it was a real Christian funeral.

Almost nine years later in the same church, in the same cemetery, we held the funeral services for my mother. This time all the prayers were in English, with white vestments. Only a few old ladies fingered rosaries silently.

Things had surely changed in the public expression of Catholic faith. (My mother, for one, always strongly supported the changes.) They deeply affected the popularity of the rosary, novenas, devotions, and processions—traditional forms of worship that were either dropped or so modified that many people became confused or lost. The result is that there is now an indifference toward, in some quarters even a disdain for, the old-time formulas.

(There is often) this supposed opposition between loving one's neighbor and loving God. Ultimately, one is not possible without the other. The two are intimately, vitally united.

Karl Rahner has confronted this problem head-on. He excludes a shallow both/and solution, but he places the horizontal and vertical directions beside each other as the two dimensions of Christian experience. A Christianity deeply conscious of its world responsibilities, he says, must still be allowed to pray, to theologize, to enjoy divine peace, to thank and praise God.

Interior prayer is vital to a human world. It is as essential to a person's humanity as the search for truth, goodness, and beauty. To live in a purely secular world of everyday work—even the work of improving social, political, and economic conditions—is deadening to the human spirit.

Let me pause here a moment to confess how difficult it is to talk about a matter so personal, so individual and private as prayer. To speak publicly about one's prayer life is like talking about one's sex life, one's love life. Maybe it's appropriate to say "love life," in a good sense, because prayer does involve someone else. Prayer is some kind of I/Thou relationship. When I speak about prayer I am not only speaking about something that is private to me; it also seems as if I am breaking a confidence with someone else.

But there is talk today of a "crisis" of prayer, and if I want to address myself to this crisis, I feel I must continue in a rather personal way.

Must one go to the mountains, into the desert or the wilderness to pray? Jesus often did so. Ten, fifteen years ago I would have laughed at the proposition that some kind of desert is a requisite for prayer. Now, I think that in some deep, special way it is in the desert, whether in a real or in a metaphoric sense, that prayer occurs.

I can remember making this discovery. Back at Saint Joseph's College in Indiana I always had music on when I was in my room.

Then I made a retreat at a Trappist monastery in Iowa. A monk-retreatmaster and I would go for walks in a kind of spiritual conference. He asked me about silence. No, I said, I don't really live with silence. I always have the radio on.

He asked whether I really listen to the radio. He suggested that I turn on the radio and listen intently to the music as long as I wanted to listen to it. Then shut it off and have silence. Eventually, I got to the point where I could, as at present, read, study, be in my room alone, completely in silence.

My relationship with nature underwent a similar transition. I always loved hunting, fishing, and vigorous hikes through the countryside. My older brother, also a priest, introduced me to the wilderness of Northern Ontario on a number of summer fishing expeditions. I always said that I liked the fishing, but I liked the country more. Eventually, I took my own words seriously. I bought myself a canoe and left the fishing gear at home. I got to the point where I liked to go canoeing alone, living along the river a week or two, with no radio, and only the sounds of nature around me.

But the change was not too easily made. My first night backpacking alone in the Sierra Nevada, was one of the loneliest nights of my life. I was not scared, just empty-alone with a fire, sleeping bag, night noises and darkness. By the second day a different fullness began to grow. Compensations come slowly but they are rewarding. Another summer evening, making camp along a small Indiana river, I had a common blackbird eat bread out of my hands.

How one does this in the city, within the rush of everyday life, I am not sure. One has to find a way, someplace, somehow. Some urban communes with their deliberate counter-culture style come close. But often, it appears, sex and drugs get in the way.

People say they like golf for the fresh air. Why not take the air without the golf? Without fear of silence or of inactivity. Without the embarrassment of admitting to doing nothing on a Sunday afternoon except finding oneself at peace.

All this may not be prayer yet. What one is trying to do is empty himself or herself in order to make it possible to become conscious of God, to put oneself in divine presence.

And this is largely physical. On this point, too, I admit to a 180-degree turn. I used to think that putting oneself in the presence of God was purely a matter of will or mind. Just sit there, turn off the body and turn on the mind, and in the "mind" you pick up God.

27

But now I feel this is a false approach. Total awareness includes the corporal, the body. The theory and practice of yoga are very much to the point here.

Finding the presence of God is something like being on a squirrel hunt, where it's necessary to sit silently for an hour or more, waiting for a squirrel to emerge from the leafy branches. In that sitting and waiting, in that learning to breathe and to make the body one with the surrounding physical universe, the smallest sounds—the shaking of a leaf, the murmur of a brook, the whistle of a bird—grow very close, almost become part of a person.

In that living consciousness of all of nature comes interior silence. And in the midst of that silence there is somehow—how should I say it? . . . can I possibly say it? As the books say, "God speaks" . . . whatever that means.

When one believes in the Incarnation—that the Word of God, the Wisdom of God became man—then one does not apologize for the physical. On the contrary one glories in the fact that the very Lord God prayed in and through the human, bodily state in which all humans must live.

Christians believe in the real living presence of God the Spirit dwelling within each of us. One element of prayer is to come in touch with and to unite oneself to the Spirit. The yogi says that one must achieve bodily equilibrium so that one's own "atman," or the individual's soul or being, becomes united to that unchanging Being which the yogis call "Brahman," or God. Christians say that one must find the real living presence of God in the Spirit which dwells within. And Christians believe that the whole physical world, including bodies, is already taken up by God in and through the sanctifying, spiritualizing activity of the Holy Spirit.

Where, then, does all this lead?

For me, the moral of the story is to return to the traditions within a Christian heritage. The riches are all here. I think this is the stage where I am now after living a year and a half within the faith of the people here high in the Central Andes of Peru. The show of religious sentiment by these Peruvians (largely a product of the Incan civilization) is not only genuine, but deeply religious in some universal sense of the word. And they are also orthodox, traditional, Christian, and Catholic. They have a sense of God, of redemption through Christ, of the Cross, and of the association of the saints with God, though they are unable to put it into words.

In my trip to India I saw the temples. I saw crowds of worshippers in different processions and practicing different modes of prayer and devotion. I was caught by conflicting emotions. One part of me wanted to participate, join them, respond to their tremendously deep religious feeling. And yet I must admit that a sense of orthodoxy—I won't say idolatry—gripped me. I couldn't feel at ease with the object of their devotion. I guess I am too thorough a Christian and a Catholic to participate unreservedly in religious practices that are thoroughly and completely non-Christian.

But here in Peru I can throw myself into the people's very public, very external practices of religion—the processions, carrying of statues, incense, the bands, the firecrackers—without reservation or fear of offending my sense of orthodoxy. A form of Catholic faith has been preserved here for four centuries. I am not here to reform it.

In many ways I find in these Peruvian customs a combination of what I have been groping for in other practices—what I think perhaps has been lost in the United States. I think some of the fervor for interiority, for transcendental meditation, for privacy of prayer (as valuable and necessary as that is) causes many Catholics to miss out on this public, corporal, communal character which is also a part of prayer.

I have to have both the interior and the public expression of prayer. I admit I can remember being embarrassed in the States when visiting certain shrines, or when participating in some gaudy Corpus Christi processions. But in truly popular and traditional religious celebrations, as among these Peruvians, there's a different experience. I feel that underneath all the spectacle and outward festivity interior prayer and worship are still going on. The communal and social seem to be combined with the divine and transcendent. This seems to happen also in prayer groups: each person prays quite privately in the noise and confusion of the whole group. When someone enters a shrine and talks publicly to Christ on the Cross, with or without others present, I consider that praying.

I remember talking to two nuns who had recently arrived in Peru. They were teaching at a high-class girls' high school. One weekend they visited one of the missions in some pueblo up along the coast. During Mass, immediately after the consecration, everything stopped for a display of fireworks and a long piece played by the band. The reaction of the sisters was not only surprise (it does take some effort to maintain composure when a whole set of popcorn firecrackers suddenly explode at one's feet); they were also shocked and offended.

But if someone really believes in the Incarnation why be shocked at such a display? If I really believe in the Mass—that somehow the words and actions of the believers and the ministering of the priests effect something physical and real over the articles of bread and wine—what should my reaction be? I could remain silent in pure awe. I could make some proclamation of faith, as the present liturgical texts ask us to do. But why not fireworks?

Once the Word of God is incarnated, thereafter the expression of one's faith, of one's inner life, is a natural, spontaneous eruption into physical, cultural things, such as dancing and fireworks.

If I believe that God is spirit alone, then everything related to God has to remain spirit. But if I am Christian and thus believe in the Incarnation, then external, physical things must be part of my expression of faith.

How to translate all this into practice in the contemporary United States I am not sure. Maybe some of the new ethnicism, with its looking backward into religious and cultural traditions, will offer some possibilities.

During the Christmas season I went to a little sleepy, nearby pueblo called Pachachaca. In the church the people had set up a tasteful crib on a portable platform they called an *anda*. Their participation was warm. They sang all the beautiful Spanish and Huayno Christmas carols.

Then, immediately after Mass, they picked up the *anda* and set it outside in the plaza, while the orchestra played native (Huayno) music. The people began a graceful dance, coming up to the crib two-by-two, in step, turning around, and coming up again.

Meanwhile, some men, the patrons of the feast, brought out two bottles of liquor and placed them at the feet of the Niño Jesús. They all had one glass apiece, poured from these bottles at the Crib of Christ and passed around to the participants. There was no embarrassment, no distinction between in church and out of church. We have the Mass, we are praying, we have the Niño Jesús with us. We dance with the Niño Jesús, we drink with the Niño Jesús. All is one living reality: who we are, what we are, what God is, and especially what we are as Christians touched by the Incarnation.

I think Catholics have all this in their past. I am not sure if some of the new fads, the new prayers are really picking this up. But I think the new liturgy can. Some celebrations I've participated in come close. Some aspects of the charismatic movement are wonderfully alive.

I began talking about a return to inner life. Yet here I am bringing up processions, dances, and fireworks, all very external things, part of very old traditions. But they must all be seen as part of a whole. Novenas worked, when they did, because they corresponded to a set of ideas about God, man, and prayer. Religious processions work here in the Central Andes of Peru because the people's faith and their community life are bound together. Yet a well-planned, well-executed Sunday liturgy in the United States may not work, because it has no real place in the everyday world of the participants. The secularized, urbanized world may be one handicap. But perhaps Western Christians also need, individually, to sit cross-legged on the floor, facing East for some time, to regain for themselves a new sense of unity of things and an understanding of why singing and dancing is important in Sunday liturgies.

For Reflection

1. What importance do the authors give to "interior prayer"? Would you agree with them or not? What does your own experience tell you of the importance of interior prayer?
2. The authors speak about listening to the radio and about silence. Describe the experience. Is silence a value in your life now? How possible is silence in our society?
3. The writers have discovered a need in their lives for interior prayer and public worship. Do you experience a similar need? How are the needs for both kinds of prayer met in your experience?
4. Why are some people called "workaholics"? Can work really become deadening to the human spirit? Rather than a prayerful spirit, what are some "substitutes" people use to escape from the pressures of their work, family, failures, and the like?
5. Reread the quotation by Konrad Lorenz in the previous section. Is there a difference between aloneness and loneliness?
6. The author says: "Total awareness includes the corporal, the body." Do you see the implications of this statement? Why do the vibrations of a "rock-beat" speak to the young? What are the importance of candles, music, etc.? Does this relate in some way to the article in Chapter 1 by Peter DeRosa?
7. Read Matthew 17:1–13. When the disciples recognized the specialness of Jesus' life, what did they want to do? What were some of their mixed emotions? What do you believe about God's presence in your life? Do you act or react accordingly?

Bibliography

Bloom, Anthony. *Living Prayer.* Springfield: Templegate, 1966.

Carroll, James. *Contemplation.* New York: Paulist Press, 1972.

DeMello, Anthony. *Sadhana: Away to God.* St. Louis: Institute of Jesuit Services, 1978.

DelBine, Ron. *A Breath of Life; A Simple Way To Pray.* Minneapolis: Winston, 1981.

Dunne, John S. *The Reasons of the Heart.* New York: Macmillan, 1974.

Eiseley, Loren. *The Star Thrower.* New York: Harcourt Brace Jovanovich, 1978.

Evely, Louis. *Teach Us How To Pray.* New York: Paulist Press, 1967.

Green, Arthur and Barry Holtz. *Your Word Is Fire.* New York: Paulist Press, 1977.

Heyer, Robert and Richard Payne. *Discovery in Prayer.* New York: Paulist Press, 1969.

Kelsey, Morton. *Dreams: A Way To Listen to God.* New York: Paulist Press, 1978.

———. *The Other Side of Silence.* New York: Paulist Press, 1976.

Link, Mark. *Breakaway.* Alton: Argus, 1980.

———. *You.* Niles: Argus Communications, 1976.

Lorenz, Konrad. *Civilized Man's Eight Deadly Sins.* New York: Harcourt Brace Jovanovich, 1974.

Nouwen, Henri J. *Pray To Live.* Notre Dame: Fides Publishers, 1972.

———. *The Way of the Heart.* New York: Ballantine, 1981.

Raines, Robert. *Lord, Could You Make It a Little Better?* Waco: Word Books, 1972.

Saint-Exupéry, Antoine de. *The Little Prince.* New York: Harcourt Brace Jovanovich, 1974.

Teilhard de Chardin, Pierre. *The Divine Milieu.* New York: Harper & Row, 1960.

Tugwell, Simon, O.P. *Prayer, Living with God.* Springfield: Templegate, 1976.

White, John, ed. *What Is Meditation?* Garden City: Anchor Books, 1974.

Chapter 3

Journal Writing: A Help in Praying

Journal Writing as a Way of Praying

People are sometimes surprised to find exercises in journal writing included in a book on prayer; but writing is an effective tool in helping us to know ourselves, especially our inner selves.

A journal is a book in which a person freely expresses whatever comes to mind or heart or spirit—without sorting out, arranging, or worrying about the choice of words or grammatical correctness. It is a tool that is personal; it reflects joys, struggles, questions, pains, and hopes as they are experienced. A journal is most helpful in reflecting what is important to an individual; it is an honest record of one's human journey.

The deepest parts of ourselves are often neglected and unknown. In our society, we tend to live on the surface. It is possible to work, eat, sleep, watch television, and even interact with people and still not be in touch with the way this is affecting us. We need techniques, such as writing, to help us reflect on and become aware of the meaning of our experiences; we need to get beneath the surface of our lives. We cannot meet God and be in touch with his love for us by living superficially.

Throughout history, people have come to know themselves and have expressed themselves through writing. Consider the psalmist David and his Old Testament prayers, Saint Augustine and his famous *Confessions,* Dag Hammarskjöld and *Markings,* Anne Frank and her *Diary of a Young Girl,* and even the four evangelists and their reflections in the Gospels on Jesus and his effect on their lives. Our journal writing can reveal our inner selves to us so that we can better share ourselves with God and those we love.

For Reflection

1. What personal writings or letters have you read that let you know the depths of the writer?
2. Have you ever been able to express in writing your dreams, your fears, or the meaning of some experience? Recall or reread that writing.

Some Observations On Journal Writing

When you write a journal, it is good to keep the following points in mind:

1. Create a quiet atmosphere so that you can get in touch with your deepest levels of thought and feeling.

2. There are no rules about what you should write; each person is free to write whatever he or she wishes. You can write about things never discussed with anyone; you can write about things that have been bothersome for some time; you can write about happy or sad things, puzzling or exciting things.

3. Any instrument or process that helps us get in touch with our deepest levels is an excellent preparation for prayer because it helps us to know the person we bring to God in prayer. Whatever helps us to know ourselves better is important for prayer.

4. We find in Matthew's Gospel the paradoxical statement: "Anyone who finds his life will lose it; anyone who loses his life for my sake will find it" (Matthew 10:39). Since the cost of losing one's life is great, a person must know and value the new life promised in this Gospel. Journal writing helps us know various dimensions of our lives and value them; the Gospel introduces us to memories of Jesus' life and its value.

5. Tensions or anxieties can keep us from prayer. By allowing them to surface in our writing, we can see them more clearly, work with them, and bring them to God in prayer—asking for mercy, help, relief or compassion. Read Psalm 142 or 86.

6. Our lives are like the passing of seasons; we have our times of spring and new life and our long, dark winters. Each unit of time in life is a small cycle containing relationships, works, goals, activities, and an image of self. Each unit has a beginning, a middle plateau, and an ending. Journal writing brings various cycles, or periods, of our lives to the surface. Seeing our belief, the God-dimension, in one or more of those cycles helps us to understand our relationship with God as it stands at the present moment.

7. A great reward of journal keeping is affirming the inner life. The dreams we have, the symbols that surface during quiet writing times, the outstanding experiences of the past that plague us or give us joy, and the deep emotion we discover in ourselves are very significant dimensions of the person we are. This inner life is the place from which prayer comes; it is where God lives in us. Can you recall a dream or a symbol that has had meaning in your life?

Praying with the Psalmist

The psalmist David was in touch with his inner life and expressed it well. He wrote his feelings in his prayers and was obviously in touch with his inner self. Listen to some of his writings. When you have time, read the complete psalm from which each of these excerpts was taken.

Psalm 22:6–8
"Yet here am I, now more worm than man,
scorn of mankind, jest of the people.
All who see me jeer at me,
they toss their heads and sneer,
'He relied on Yahweh, let Yahweh save him!' "

Psalm 63:1–2
"God, you are my God, I am seeking you,
my soul is thirsting for you,
My flesh is longing for you,
a land parched, weary and waterless."

Psalm 131:1–2
"Yahweh, my heart has no lofty ambitions,
my eyes do not look too high.
I am not concerned with great affairs
or marvels beyond my scope.
Enough for me to keep my soul tranquil and quiet
like a child in its mother's arms,
as content as a child that has been weaned."

Psalm 116:10–11
"I have faith, even when I say,
'I am completely crushed.'
In my alarm, I declared,
'No man can be relied on.' "

Psalm 133:1
"How good, how delightful it is
for all to live together like brothers."

David found words to express his delight, his faith, his longing, and desire; he found images to express distress—"more worm than man" and "jest of the people"—and images to express his trust—"quiet like a child in its mother's arms." Expressing in writing what is deep within us, freely and honestly as David did, will be helpful in revealing ourselves to our God. The Gospels themselves can be seen as journals: written memories of the words, activities, struggles and triumphs of Jesus. The journals of his life are words with power that we listen to in order to know him well; our journal writings, too, can reveal our inner selves to us. Prayer involves mutual self-revelation; we listen to God, and we share ourselves with him.

For Reflection

Use the following to initiate your journal writing.

1. What are the feelings expressed in the psalms?
2. Restate the psalms in contemporary language.
3. Identify the feelings of the psalmist which reflect your own.

A Time in My Life

Directions: Select a time in your life during the last six months or during any six-month period that was very important to you and that you remember well. Write a short paragraph about that period, beginning "It was a time when. . . ." Include in your paragraph the way things were going for you and how you felt.

_____

_____

_____

_____

_____

_____

_____

Now go on to the chart, which will help you surface specific things about this time in your life.

Example:

	Subject	*Feelings*	*Comment*	*Question*
Person	Mary	I appreciate her sensitivity	She went out of her way for me	I wonder if she realized how much I needed her
Event	Realizing I was very lonely	Helpless	I thought life held nothing for me	I wonder why we are so unprepared to lose someone through death

A Time In My Life

From _____ To _____

	Subject	Feelings about Persons, work, etc.	Comment about each	Question you would now ask of each
Persons				
Work				
Events				
Activities				
Materials read				
Religious experience				

Reflections on the Psalms

Thinking about these words in the psalmist's life can assist you in writing further reflections on memorable or ordinary times in your own life.

Psalm 84:1–2, 4–5
"How I love your palace,
    Yahweh Sabaoth!
How my soul yearns and pines
    for Yahweh's courts!
My heart and my flesh sing for joy
    to the living God.
Happy those who live in your house
    and can praise you all day long;
And happy the pilgrims inspired by you
    with courage to make the Ascents!"

Psalm 86:1–2, 11–13
"Listen to me, Yahweh, and answer me,
    poor and needy as I am;
Keep my soul: I am your devoted one;
    save your servant who relies on you.
Yahweh, teach me your way,
    how to walk beside you faithfully,
    make me single-hearted in fearing your name.
I thank you with all my heart, Lord my God.
    I glorify your name for ever,
Your love for me has been so great,
    you have rescued me from the depths of Sheol."

Psalm 89:1–2
"I will celebrate your love for ever, Yahweh,
    age after age my words shall proclaim your faithfulness;
For I claim that love is built to last for ever
    and your faithfulness founded firmly in the heavens."

Psalm 102:1–2
"Yahweh, hear my prayer,
    let my cry for help reach you;
Do not hide your face from me
    when I am in trouble;
Bend down to listen to me,
    when I call, be quick to answer me!"

Psalm 139:1–3
"Yahweh, you examine me and know me;
    you know if I am standing or sitting,
    you read my thoughts from far away.
Whether I walk or lie down, you are watching,
    you know every detail of my conduct."

For Reflection in Your Journal
1. How do these psalms relate to my life?
2. What phrases appeal to me and why?
3. How do I celebrate God's love?
4. For what things do I cry to Yahweh?

Using the Scriptures for Journal Writing

Select three periods for prayer. In each of those periods, read the selected Scripture slowly. Reflect on the Scripture briefly in the manner suggested, and write in your journal.

1. *Luke 10:1–10, 17–20* Surprise
Reflect on the feelings of the apostles, especially their feelings of apprehension and surprise when Jesus sent them on their mission and when they reported back to Jesus. In your journal, write a paragraph that relates a new or remembered experience of the unexpected, a surprise that was a positive experience for you.

2. *John 21:4–14* Celebration
Read the passage slowly. Put yourself in the shoes of the apostles. How did they feel? What kind of remarks do you think they made? Write a paragraph, beginning "Once I was a part of a celebration that. . . ."

3. *Luke 7:1–10* Healing
Read the passage slowly. Reflect on the conversation. What moved Jesus to heal? How are you like the centurion? How are you different? Write a paragraph in which you recall and describe a healing of body, mind, spirit, or memory that made it possible for you to continue your life in a better way.

Bibliography
Baum, Gregory, ed. *Journeys*. New York: Paulist Press, 1975.
Guzie, Tad. *The Book of Sacramental Basics*. New York: Paulist Press, 1981.
Higgins, John J. *Merton's Theology of Prayer*. New York: Doubleday, 1975.
Kelsey, Morton. *Dreams: A Way To Listen to God*. New York: Paulist Press, 1978.
McMahon, J.J. *Between You and You*. New York: Paulist Press, 1980.
Nouwen, Henri. *In Memoriam*. Notre Dame: Ave Maria Press, 1980.
———. *The Genesee Diary*. Garden City: Doubleday, 1976.
Progoff, Ira. *At a Journal Workshop*. New York: Dialogue House Library, 1975.
———. *The Well and the Cathedral*. New York: Dialogue House Library, 1972.
Shea, John. *Stories of God*. Chicago: Thomas More Press, 1978.
Simons, George. *Keeping Your Personal Journal*. New York: Paulist Press, 1978.
Vanier, Jean. *Followers of Jesus*. New York: Paulist Press, 1976.
Vetter, Bernadette. *My Journey, My Prayer*. New York: Sadlier, 1977.

Chapter 4

Praying with Scripture

Praying with Scripture

Scripture is a source of great inspiration and assistance in prayer. It is possible to come to the Scriptures simply as an interested reader or with the knowledge and tools of a biblical scholar. Our approach to Scripture, however, will be to treat it as a source of prayer, as the word of God that can touch us and change us.

We can focus on what Scripture tells us about the faith-journey of Jesus and about his relationship with the Father, his disciples, and those he met and to whom he ministered.

It is possible to read the story of the rich young man or the Samaritan woman and imagine ourselves to be in their shoes. How would we respond? What thoughts and feelings would surface in us?

One can pray the psalms of David and find expressed in them almost every human feeling. Psalm 139 is a good psalm to begin with in prayer; it expresses how completely God knows us and how deeply he cares for us.

Frequently, what we need most when we come to pray is to quiet down, to center ourselves. A given line in Scripture can assist us in doing that. Choose a line such as "Be still and know that I am God" or "I have loved you with an everlasting love"; relax, breathe deeply, and repeat the line slowly and reflectively.

These are a few suggestions for beginning your meditation with the Scriptures. You will discover other ways of your own. Sometimes Scripture may seem dry and uninteresting; at other times it will initiate a profound experience or a deep insight. Being faithful to it can lead us to an encounter with God.

For Reflection

1. Do you have a favorite passage in Scripture? How has it touched you? What meaning does it hold for you?

2. Can you recall a powerful homily or talk you heard on a passage of Scripture? What insight did the speaker give that made the talk memorable for you?

Jesus, A Faithful Jew

In order to discover the richness of the Gospels for prayer, we must reflect on Jesus—his heritage, his use of scripture, and his legacy.

If we are to enter into an understanding of the real, human Jesus—what he was like, how he thought—the first thing we must recognize is that Jesus was a Jew! He was born a Jew; he was reared a Jew; he was steeped in Jewish tradition. Jesus was called the Nazarene; he was the son of Mary and Joseph of the family of David.

What this means is that Jesus was steeped in the Old Testament, the Hebrew Bible; he was thoroughly familiar with the Hebrew scriptural concepts. As a child he prayed with Mary and

Joseph, the local rabbi, neighbors, friends, and relatives by reciting, listening to, and meditating on the Hebrew Scriptures. And what did those scriptures say?

A fundamental teaching of the Old Testament is that God the Father truly entered people's destiny. By his covenant, or pact, with Abraham and all the great patriarchs, God became an integral part of Humanity's life and history.

God did more than enter history, however; he directed it. From the Scriptures we learn, as Jesus learned, that God touches our lives constantly—giving them direction and order. Unlike the pagan gods, whom people used and created to serve their own purposes, the God of Israel demanded that his people serve him. He promised to give their lives meaning if they served him. They would belong to him and he would belong to them! They would be "holy," that is "set apart" as the people of the Lord.

The Old Testament also teaches that God the Father relates to people through prayer and worship. The destiny of Israel was to attain perfect union with Yahweh through unqualified submission to his will; and only then could Israel attain peace and salvation.

Since Jesus was Jewish, he loved his people, his traditions, his ancestors, and his God. But he was rejected. Why? The insights and understanding Jesus came to by praying with the Scriptures deemphasized externals and emphasized an interiorization of God's Law, but this did not always work in Jesus' favor.

Christianity is concerned about the person of Christ. The New Testament describes a man who had emotions, who hungered and thirsted for justice, as well as for food and drink; a man who tired himself out for others. He was not only descended from the family of David, but he taught with authority. He was not only the prophet descended from the royal family, but he fulfilled the description of Isaiah—he is the suffering servant—a man acquainted with inequities. And he was the one who offered himself to God.

Early Christianity was also concerned about the words and deeds of Jesus. Pondering the Scriptures and interacting with others in friendship and service, Jesus asked himself the same question we ask ourselves: who am I in the plan of God? Thus the Jewish concept found its fulfillment in Jesus—that God is my life. I have a mission; that is, God directs my life and he will make known what is necessary for me, through prayer and worship.

In his letters to the Galatians and to the Romans, Saint Paul made a very important point relating to our theme. The basic concepts of Jewish thinking have been passed on not just by the passing on of physical life through physical generation. It is not just the semitic stock that transfers the "chosen"ness, not just Jewish blood alone.

What is it then? FAITH! Abraham, the father of the chosen race, was the first one who came to believe and trust in the one God. Jesus is *fully* alive, fully human, because of this *full faith* in God, because of his *faithful* response to the heritage passed down by those who preceded him. His Jewish background, his heritage, accounted for certain influences in his thinking, yet his descent was more by way of Spirit (faith—the power of faith) than by blood.

By being open to the Jewish Scriptures, by praying the Jewish Scriptures, Jesus discovered through quiet, study, meditation and worshipful celebration that God truly was alive in him, directing his life and present to him.

John the Evangelist wrote: "In the beginning was the Word, and the Word was with God and the Word was God. . . . The Word was made flesh, he lived among us" (John 1:1, 14). Praying with the scriptures in a spirit of openness and obedience will do no less for us: the word of God will take flesh in our lives too. Prayer will enable the God-likeness in us to shine forth. It will help us to recognize God in our lives. It will enable us to understand the mission and destiny of our lives, the healing and hallowing presence of God here and now. In this sense, praying with the Scriptures will allow the Word of God, the living person of Jesus, to become flesh in each of our lives.

For Reflection

1. Was Jesus' life and destiny all laid out for him as though he carried a blueprint of his identity and mission? What were some of the risks that Jesus faced in the process of self-discovery and in carrying out his mission in life?

2. In what ways do you think the life of Jesus and our own lives are similar? What are some questions that Jesus must have asked in his life that we should also ask in our lives?

3. Jesus' Jewish genealogy was extremely important to his mission and destiny, but it was realized only through prayer, struggle, and reflection. How does this relate to our lives?

4. Jesus was becoming aware of his mission by relating to others, as well as by meditating on the Scriptures. Give examples of Jesus' interaction with others. What did he learn from others? How are we like Jesus? Jesus' prayer never centered exclusively on "God and me"; rather he made it a part of his daily life. This should also be true of our prayer. Explain. Give examples.

Using Scripture to Pray

I. Sometimes the primary need in prayer is to quiet down, to center ourselves, to let the cares and concerns of the day fall away for a short time. The repetition of a line from Scripture or the Jesus Prayer can be of help. To pray this way, choose a line; relax, breathe deeply; and repeat the line slowly and quietly. The following are some appropriate lines for prayer:

"Pause a while and know that I am God" (Psalm 46:10).

"I have loved you with an everlasting love" (Jeremiah 31:3).

"Your sins are forgiven" (Luke 7:48).

"O Lord Jesus Christ, Son of God,
have mercy on me, a sinner" (Jesus Prayer).

"You are precious in my eyes" (Isaiah 43:4).

On some days, the repetition of a line can be an introduction to your prayer; on other days, you can spend the entire time of prayer simply repeating the line, reflecting on it.

II. Sometimes it is good to take a very familiar section of Scripture and read it to see if you find new meaning in it. The story of the prodigal son, for example, is familiar, but did you every try to understand and identify with the older son in the story? The story of the temptation in the desert is also one that all of us know. But we can deepen our understanding of the story by considering the temptation episode as a struggle for Jesus between being the kind of Messiah he knew through reflection and prayer he must be and being the kind of Messiah the people wanted him to be. Familiar passages can speak to us in a new way when we come to them with open hearts.

III. One line of Scripture can frequently serve as the basis for our reflection. Consider, for example, the profound meaning of the following line:
"My food is to do the will of the one who sent me" (John 4:34).
The following questions might stimulate our reflection and help us understand this line of Scripture:

- What does food do?
- What happens when one's food is the Father's will?
- How did it nourish Jesus?
- How can it nourish me?
- What does this say about dependency on God?

IV. Ask yourself these questions. They will give you some idea of the power of Scripture, the word of God.

- Have you ever had a *word* purify you as fire? Or as people might say today, have words ever pressed you to be painfully honest?
- Have you ever had a *word* destroy hardness of heart like a strong hammer, or break through your prejudice and lead you to accept someone you had previously shunned?
- Have you ever felt a *word* penetrate like a sword through your defenses to the truth in your heart, and open your life to someone else?
- Have you had a *word* cause desire and love to burn in your heart?
- Have the *words* of a story ever led you to tears, and/or motivated you to extend your hand to others?

Praying as Participation in God's Work

If we truly enter into the Scriptures through prayer, we will begin to recognize the most significant mystery of life, the rhythm or relationship between the human and divine.

In the Old Testament we see the godly qualities of faithfulness and obedience in Abraham and the human qualities of friendship and concern in Yahweh, who spoke to Moses "as a friend speaks to a friend." The psalms cry out with human qualities—sinfulness and repentance—as

well as the divine qualities of majesty, fidelity, acceptance, and forgiveness. In the New Testament, we see Jesus as one of us, burdened with the same problems that touch us, and yet he was both human and divine.

The more deeply we enter into the Scriptures, the more deeply we enter into a profound mystery: humanity's relationship to divinity—a mystery that philosophers, theologians, artists, writers, statesmen, and ordinary, everyday people like us must enter into if we choose life and live it fully.

In his novel, *The Honorary Consul,* Graham Greene has one of his characters, Leon Rivas, say:

"The God I believe in must be responsible for all the evil as well as for all the saints. He has to be a God made in our image with a night-side as well as a day-side. . . . I believe the time will come when the night-side will wither away . . . and we shall see only the simple daylight of the good God. You believe in evolution, Eduardo, even though sometimes whole generations of men slip backwards to the beasts. It is a long struggle and a long suffering evolution, and I believe God is suffering the same evolution that we are, but perhaps with more pain. . . . The evolution of God depends on our evolution. Every evil act of ours strengthens his night-side, and every good one strengthens his day-side. We belong to him and he belongs to us. But now at least we can be sure where evolution will end one day—it will end in a goodness like Christ's."

There are many things that could be said about the above quotation, but two points should suffice for our purpose here. One is that Jesus, in his goodness, is the personification—the incarnation—of the human and divine. The other is that we are called to an *intimate participation* in the mystery of the incarnation.

The incarnation was described by St. John in the opening verses of his Gospel. The Word of God became flesh; "he lived among us" (John 1:14). The reality of Christmas is that God became more visible. At the exodus God had committed himself to be part of our quest, ultimately to become one of us. In his Gospel, John clearly states the meaning of the incarnation— Jesus was truly man; Jesus was truly God. We see Jesus celebrating at the wedding feast of Cana, venting his anger at the money-changers in the temple, asking a Samaritan woman (in an act forbidden by law) for a drink of water, weeping, groaning, worrying, and washing his disciples' feet. At other times, we are made aware of Jesus' divinity. He considers himself the Father's ambassador, possessing the Father's power and works (John 5:19–24. 36–38). We read in John 6: "I am the living bread which came down from heaven. Anyone who eats this bread will live forever" (John 6:51). And again in John 8: "He who sent me is with me, and has not left me to myself, for I always do what pleases him. . . . I tell you most solemnly, before Abraham ever was, I Am!" (John 8:29. 58).

In his little book *Loose in the World,* Thomas O'Meara offers a keen insight which might be helpful as we pray the Scriptures:

The early followers of Christ through public wordsmithing became known as Christians, just as communists are known as Marxists. The assignment of a successful Marxist is not to reproduce exactly either the life or the teaching of Karl Marx, but to forge a revolutionary economical system. Similarly, those who find in Christ the concrete presence of what they can discover in their own lives may not describe themselves well when they sum up their entire identities by the name "Christians." For me to live in presence is not to have a collective name, to submit to an ideology, an "—ism." We are not interested in "Christians" any more than in "religious" people, for they, we suspect, may have abandoned the real world.

The best follower of Christ is not the man or woman who, pondering over the Gospels, does nothing more or less than what Jesus actually did or would do if he were alive in Seattle at this moment. It is impossible to live in America and to look up precise patterns in the Gospel for the actions of each day. Gospels are as fragmentary as they are powerful. Christianity has long been plagued by the dead weight of the imitation of Christ.

When Jesus Christ is seen as the person where the *transcendence of man* meets the light of God, then that meeting can be pondered and lived out. But when the imitation of Christ becomes lost in neurotic uncertainties over how Jesus did or did not behave, in bizarre attempts to be "Christ-like," superstition results. Literal religion deforms people and makes the future ugly.

The plan of God for us in history does not call us to be other Jesus Christs, for we are unique individuals. Jesus does suggest that we learn about him as well as from him, but his response to blustering Peter or wealthy Joseph of Arimathea is that they become themselves. "Become?" Personal development does not end on a comfortable plateau easily within my capabilities. Real humanism must stimulate the mysterious factor we call presence, balance the questioning and the proclivity for mistakes in all men and women. Becoming myself is at the same time offering myself to a mystery beyond me. The goal of grace is person. We are called, then, not so much to be Catholics or Christians, not communists or Africans, Buddhists or Americans, but to walk with eyes alert for the ambience of grace around our life. Then we can fashion out of pain and joy a life which lasts.

The scientist, philosopher, and inventor Buckminster Fuller puts it another way. To paraphrase him: I am not just a noun—a static thing; I seem to be a verb—alive and moving. And even though I may be small and insignificant, I am like that little pin in the rudder of a great ship—*essential* to moving the ship in whatever direction the captain desires. In a similar way, our participation in the incarnation is like that pin. We are essential to moving God's work and presence in our world forward toward the omega point.

A number of authors, such as Andrew Greeley and Eugene Kennedy, have pointed out the benefits and dangers, the strengths and weaknesses of a personalistic age. But they are quick to tell us that we are individuals enhanced with a wonderful dignity and ability to become a part of the Lord's living revelation to mankind.

We know that the books of Scripture are both a record of concrete events and a "process" that illustrates the plan of the Father. Jesus makes life and grace *concrete* and the spirit becomes a probing milieu which surrounds me. Jesus' words and deeds do not dictate a program. Rather they encourage me and help me to visualize, to relate, and to compare. What we do, therefore, increases the possibilities and range of God's activity. It also propels us more deeply and consciously into the experience of shared life with God. The Lord calls us to an encounter with him, welcomes our participation in his life, and enters with us into a relationship that is energizing for the whole living Church, and indeed for all of creation.

With this kind of understanding of God's presence, activity and friendship, and our participation in his work, we can go on searching the Scriptures prayerfully, allowing them to touch our experiences and to move us to a deeper involvement with God.

For Reflection

1. Read one or two chapters of John's Gospel slowly and prayerfully. Notice how often he joins the human and divine in Jesus. If several groups would like to discuss John's Gospel together, each group could cover a few chapters and share their insights with one another. They could meditate together on the Gospel over a period of time.

2. When you read any of the books of the Bible, choose a character that strikes you as interesting. Try to enter into the passage. Figure out the similarities or differences between you and the character you have chosen. What thoughts and feelings does that person and the situation strike in you at this moment of your life?

3. As you use the Scriptures, remember Fr. O'Meara's insight that the Scriptures are illustrations of the mysterious meeting between the human and divine. We do not copy or attempt to become identical replicas of biblical characters. Rather, we allow them to inspire whatever is unique and given to us by God so that we can more fully enter into the presence of grace around us.

Scriptural Meditation

Method of Prayer

1. Breathe deeply and try to get yourself completely quiet and composed. Let all the things that are on your mind come to you and place them in God's hands. Call to mind that you are in the presence of God and say a brief prayer asking the Father, Son, and Holy Spirit to help you in your prayer.

2. Read Luke 7:36–50.

3. Put yourself into the Gospel scene at the dinner. Make yourself present there. Try to feel what Jesus, or the woman, or Simon felt. Listen to their conversation.

4. Have you found yourself in difficult situations? Have you ever felt emotion so strongly that you had to express it, as the woman here had to find a way to express her gratitude and love? Did you ever forgive or receive forgiveness from another and have that experience become an important memory? Do you experience God's forgiveness and love? Is there someone you need to forgive? Is there someone you wish to ask for forgiveness?

5. End the prayer time with your own words to God about yourself, this passage, your God and your relationship to others.

6. Jot down in your journal a sentence describing how you felt during your prayer and another sentence or two stating what you think God is saying to you through this Gospel story.

Bibliography
Bednarski, Sister Gloriana, R.S.M. *Listening for the Lord.* Mystic: Twenty-Third Publications, 1977.
Bruggemann, Walter. *The Bible Makes Sense.* Atlanta: John Knox Press, 1978.
Donders, Joseph. *Jesus, Heaven on Earth.* Maryknoll: Orbis Books, 1980.
Greene, Graham. *The Honorary Consul.* New York: Simon & Schuster, 1973.
LaVerdiere, Eugene A., S.S.S. *Trumpets of Beaten Metal.* Collegeville: Liturgical Press, 1974.
Link, Mark, S.J. *The Mustard Seed.* Niles: Argus Communications, 1974.
Martin, George. *Reading Scripture as the Word of God.* Ann Arbor: Word of Life, 1975.
Morrow, Stanley B. *The Words of Jesus in Our Gospels.* New York: Paulist Press, 1979.
O'Meara, Thomas, O.P. *Loose in the World.* New York: Paulist Press, 1974.
Sanford, John. *The Kingdom Within.* New York: Paulist Press, 1970.
Senior, Donald, C.P. *Jesus: A Gospel Portrait.* Cincinnati: Pflaum/Standard, 1975.

Chapter 5

Faith-Development Through Prayer

Faith-Development

All of us who are concerned about praying are on a journey in faith. At times it is exciting, and we are aware of our spiritual development; other times are difficult and dark. All of the periods and events of our lives, however, can be invitations to develop a closer relationship with God and the Christian community.

In *Cuthman,* a play by Christopher Fry, a young Christian shepherd experiences a personal tragedy that calls him to mature faith. When Cuthman hears of his father's death, he is crushed. The chorus in the play calls out the line, "How is your faith now, Cuthman, your faith that the warm world hatched?" Before the sudden death of his father, Cuthman's faith had been nourished ("hatched") in the warm world of family, friends, and community. Now his faith was being challenged to grow through crisis. Our faith is also challenged by daily events. The outcome depends on how we *see* what happens in our lives. Cuthman eventually came to see even the death of his father as a way to grow in his relationship with God.

In his treatment of moral and religious maturity, author James Fowler has suggested that there are six stages that people go through in life as they develop their faith. It is not until the third stage that the individual's world moves beyond the family. During the fourth stage, the person of religious faith experiences certain tensions and conflicts in values. When he or she knows the value and meaning of defeat and failure, the fifth stage of development has been reached.

51

During the course of *Cuthman,* we see the young shepherd move from stage four to stage five of faith development—to the level of mature faith. The sixth and final stage, that of universalizing faith, is generally achieved by great leaders, those totally fulfilled individuals whose own security can threaten the insecurities of many other people. That stage will be more evident as we reflect on Peter the Apostle.

Peter's story was one of deepening trust in Jesus, the Father, and the Holy Spirit. His development during the years of Jesus' ministry prepared him to be a faith-filled leader of the first Christian community. Let us look more closely at that faith-development by pursuing the story of Peter.

The circumstances of his call were a little overwhelming. He and his companions had fished all night long without success—until Jesus ordered them to lower their nets. And then they caught more than they could handle. With that, Peter blurted out in honesty, "Leave me, Lord; I am a sinful man." With a little encouragement, however, he was willing to enter into a relationship with Jesus. On the day he was called, Peter became a listener, a believer, a follower of Jesus.

As he listened to and observed Jesus, his faith deepened; on one occasion he even tried to walk on the water to reach Jesus. He recognized Jesus as the Messiah and ministered with him. Although Peter was growing in his faith, he later dramatized his weakness when he denied Jesus. But immediately there was repentance and forgiveness. The healing of the wound caused by denial was begun.

After the resurrection, Jesus was very gentle with Peter and completed the healing process with his repeated question, "Peter, do you love me?" He affirmed Peter by giving him the ministry to lead the Christian people when he said, "Feed my lambs. . . . Feed my sheep."

There is much to reflect on in the story of Peter. We see his strengths and weaknesses and his growth in faith. We are involved in a similar growth process. Like Peter, we can find strength and help for this growth in our prayer-relationship with Jesus, the Father and the Holy Spirit and in our interactions with one another in the Christian community.

The Call of the Apostles

Jesus Calls Peter, James and John (Luke 5:1–11)

"Now he was standing one day by the Lake of Gennesaret, with the crowd pressing round him listening to the word of God, when he caught sight of two boats close to the bank. The fishermen had gone out of them and were washing their nets. He got into one of the boats—it was Simon's—and asked him to put out a little from the shore. Then he sat down and taught the crowds from the boat.

"When he had finished speaking he said to Simon, 'Put out into deep water and put out your nets for a catch.' 'Master,' Simon replied, 'we worked hard all night long and caught nothing, but if you say so, I will put out the nets.' And when they had done this they netted such a huge number of fish that their nets began to tear, so they signalled to their companions in the other boat to come and help them; when these came, they filled the two boats to sinking point.

"When Simon Peter saw this he fell at the knees of Jesus saying, 'Leave me, Lord; I am a sinful man.' For he and all his companions were completely overcome by the catch they had made; so also were James and John, sons of Zebedee, who were Simon's partners. But Jesus said to Simon, 'Do not be afraid; from now on it is men you will catch.' Then, bringing their boats back to land, they left everything and followed him."

A Commentary

According to Luke's account of the call, Peter followed the Lord's request to put out the fishing nets again. The result was a good catch. Peter trusted Jesus' request and was made aware by what happened that in Jesus there was more than meets the eye. A little afraid, he blurted out, "Leave me, Lord; I am a sinful man." He had an insight into himself; he was also touched deeply by the person of Jesus. He saw a mystery in this event.

Jesus' response was one he often made, "Do not be afraid": do not be afraid of my power, of mystery, of your own sinfulness. That day Peter became a listener, a believer, a follower of the one who knows the Father and his mission. He entered into a profound relationship with Jesus that would be a commitment for life. Peter brought his weakness and his honesty with him. His awareness of Jesus as one who brings light to the darkness of human existence would become more intense. He would want to know more. Peter was attracted to Jesus and was willing to give himself completely to this relationship. This was the beginning stage of Peter's faith. As an adult coming to faith, he recognized the goodness and power of Jesus. In trust, he followed him.

For Reflection
1. Reflect on the mysterious aspect of Peter's call, his feelings, his uncertainty, his willingness to risk. Think about your willingness to risk. Think about your own call to a relationship with God, your vocation to be Christian. How has it evolved over the years through prayer and your experiences of life?
2. Notice that Jesus' invitation to follow him is immediately related to others. His disciples will be made fishers and their "catch" will be new disciples. How has your Christian vocation compelled you to be the good news for others?
3. What has moved you to trust in others and in God?

Peter Attempts To Walk on Water (Matthew 14:22–23)
"Directly after this he made the disciples get into the boat and go on ahead to the other side while he would send the crowds away. After sending the crowds away he went up into the hills by himself to pray. When evening came, he was there alone, while the boat, by now far out on the lake, was battling with a heavy sea, for there was a head-wind. In the fourth watch of the night he went towards them, walking on the lake, and when the disciples saw him walking on the lake they were terrified. 'It is a ghost,' they said, and cried out in fear. But at once Jesus called out to them, saying, 'Courage! It is I! Do not be afraid.' It was Peter who answered. 'Lord,' he said, 'if it is you, tell me to come to you across the water.' 'Come,' said Jesus. Then Peter got out of the boat and started walking towards Jesus across the water, but as soon as he felt the force of the wind, he took fright and began to sink. 'Lord! Save me!' he cried. Jesus put out his hand at once and held him. 'Man of little faith,' he said, 'why did you doubt?' And as they got into the boat the wind dropped. The men in the boat bowed down before him and said, 'Truly, you are the Son of God.''

A Commentary

After observing Jesus in his teaching and healing ministries, Peter was conscious of an unusual power in this preacher who had invited him to be a disciple. He was ready to trust him—even to take risks, if necessary. On the occasion described in this passage, the disciples were fearful; but Jesus assured them when he said, "Courage! It is I! Do not be afraid." Jesus invited Peter to join him, and he tried; he stepped out of the boat onto the dark, deep waters. His faith was strong enough for him to take the risk, but "as soon as he felt the force of the wind, he took fright and began to sink." In this dangerous situation, he was filled with fear, but he had sense enough to call out, "Lord, save me." He knew he needed help. Jesus gently reprimanded him: "Man of little faith, why did you doubt?" He taught him faith by pointing out his doubt. Peter learned from his experience of trying to walk on water. He then knew something about courage, about risk, about strength, about weakness, about faith, about doubt and about the power of Jesus.

For Reflection

1. Can you remember "storms" in your life, times when the boat was rocking and you were fearful?
2. What do you see as the role of doubt in this story? How did Jesus respond to it? Theologians say doubt is necessary in growth toward a mature faith. Can you recall instances in your life in which doubt was present and, perhaps, threatening?
3. Can you remember times when you listened to others as they shared the storms and difficulties of their lives? How did you try to help them?

Peter's Profession of Faith (Matthew 16:13–20)

"When Jesus came to the region of Caesarea Philippi he put this question to his disciples, 'Who do people say the Son of Man is?' And they said, 'Some say he is John the Baptist, some Elijah, and others Jeremiah or one of the prophets.' 'But you,' he said, 'who do you say I am?' Then Simon Peter spoke up, 'You are the Christ,' he said, 'the Son of the living God.' Jesus replied, 'Simon son of Jonah, you are a happy man! Because it was not flesh and blood that revealed this to you but my Father in heaven. So I now say to you: You are Peter and on this rock I will build my Church. And the gates of the underworld can never hold out against it. I will give you the keys to the kingdom of heaven: whatever you bind on earth shall be considered bound in heaven; whatever you loose on earth shall be considered loosed in heaven.' Then he gave the disciples strict orders not to tell anyone that he was the Christ."

A Commentary

Peter recognized in some way Jesus' messiahship and responded as a firm believer. Jesus made an interesting statement about Peter's insight and understanding—that flesh and blood did not reveal this to Peter, but his Father. It was not books, nor observation of events, nor even listening to Jesus' words, but a greater power that revealed Jesus' identity and gave Peter the power to believe. Peter was in some way listening to the Father's will in his life as he came to know Jesus, the Son of the living God. Jesus' response was again the type that builds trust. He called Peter to a deeper commitment: "I will give you the keys of the kingdom of heaven. . . ." Although it still was not clear to Peter what Jesus' identity would mean in terms of suffering, he had reached a new level of faith. Our faith development is in many ways a matter of seeing—seeing more clearly, more fully, more deeply. Prayer and a relationship with Jesus enabled Peter to "see" Jesus as the Messiah.

For Reflection

1. Reflect on Peter's insight that Jesus was the Messiah. What did this mean to Peter? To Jesus? Can you recall having an insight about yourself, or another, or a situation that has really affected your life? Can you remember something that helped you "see" a truth to which you had been blind?

2. Reflect on your faith-life as it is now and as it was five years ago. If you think it is the same, why is that so? What contributes to growth and change in faith? How are members of the Christian community involved in your growth? How does growth in faith make us more conscious of all people as our brothers and sisters?

Peter's Denial (Luke 22:31–34. 54–62)

" 'Simon, Simon! Satan, you must know, has got his wish to sift you all like wheat; but I have prayed for you, Simon, that your faith may not fail, and once you have recovered, you in your turn must strengthen your brothers.' 'Lord,' he answered, 'I would be ready to go to prison with you, and to death.' Jesus replied, 'I tell you, Peter, by the time the cock crows today you will have denied three times that you know me.'

"They seized him then and led him away, and they took him to the high priest's house. Peter followed at a distance. They had lit a fire in the middle of the courtyard and Peter sat down among them, and as he was sitting there by the blaze a servant-girl saw him, peered at him, and said, 'This person was with him too.' But he denied it. 'Woman,' he said, 'I do not know him.' Shortly afterwards someone else saw him and said, 'You are another of them.' But Peter replied, 'I am not, my friend.' About an hour later another man insisted, saying, 'This fellow was certainly with him. Why, he is a Galilean.' 'My friend,' said Peter, 'I do not know what you are talking about.' At that instant, while he was still speaking, the cock crew, and the Lord turned and looked straight at Peter, and Peter remembered what the Lord had said to him, 'Before the cock crows today, you will have disowned me three times.' And he went outside and wept bitterly."

A Commentary

It becomes clear in this event that sin does not make us into non-believers. In fact, in some mysterious way, Peter's experience of denial and the encounter with Jesus that followed were important steps for Peter toward the development of mountain-moving faith. St. Luke emphasizes the outcome: "And once you have recovered, you, in your turn, must strengthen your brothers." He wants to make us aware of Jesus' radical kind of forgiveness that is always available to us. In the denial account, the moment and method of forgiveness are made clear: "The Lord turned and looked straight at Peter, and Peter remembered. . . ." In the encounter of love and forgiveness, and in the memory of the prediction, the love and the friendship of Jesus were both present. The encounter and the memory were redemptive. Peter was open to receive forgiveness and was filled with the awareness of his weakness; he wept bitterly.

1. Reflect on the Lord looking straight at Peter and on the thoughts and feelings both must have experienced. Can you remember moments of great pain and great forgiveness in your life?
2. Reflect radical example of forgiveness that Jesus gives here. Can we forgive those who hurt us? Do we contribute to strengthening those in our home, parish, or community in gratitude for God's loving forgiveness of us?

"Peter, Do You Love Me?" (John 21:15–19)

"After the meal Jesus said to Simon Peter, 'Simon son of John, do you love me more than these others do?' He answered, 'Yes, Lord, you know I love you.' Jesus said to him, 'Feed my lambs.' A second time he said to him, 'Simon son of John, do you love me?' He replied, 'Yes, Lord, you know I love you.' Jesus said to him, 'Look after my sheep.' Then he said to him a third time, 'Simon son of John, do you love me?' Peter was upset that he asked him the third time 'Do you love me?' and said, 'Lord, you know everything; you know I love you.' Jesus said to him,

> 'Feed my sheep.
> I tell you most solemnly,
> when you were young
> you put on your own belt
> and walked where you liked;
> but when you grow old
> you will stretch out your hands,
> and somebody else will put a belt round you
> and take you where you would rather not go.'

In these words he indicated the kind of death by which Peter would give glory to God. After this he said, 'Follow me.' "

A Commentary

This event was a healing experience for Peter. Jesus' triple questioning heightened Peter's consciousness of the denial event and brought those feelings to the surface again. Peter's earlier statement that he did not know Jesus was a denial of his relationship with him. Now Jesus was asking him to reaffirm that relationship by acknowledging the bonds of love between them. The pain of the healing experience and the depth of Peter's love are seen in his words, "Lord, you know everything; you know I love you." Jesus accepted Peter's love and faith and affirmed him by asking him to keep his position as head of the Church: "Feed my lambs. . . . Feed my sheep." After this, Jesus said again, "Follow me," and Peter, now more mature in his faith, followed Jesus faithfully even unto death. At the end of this story, Peter's faith was well developed. He was ready to commit himself to Jesus and to loving others—even to the point of laying down his own life.

For Reflection

1. In order for deep wounds to be healed, we need to remember them and feel again the pain they caused; after that, we can let go of them. This story invites us to look at our past and not be afraid to see what needs healing in us. Can we open our wounded life-experiences to God's healing love?

2. Think about the confidence Jesus had in Peter, even after the denial. Do we believe that God always accepts us and trusts us to help ("to feed") his people?

A Meditation

Read and reflect on the following passage, and then put aside some time to use the other two references for a similar meditation. Always listen closely to the words of Scripture before you begin to think or write a response in your journal.

Read John 13:1–15. Then read the following personal reflection.

I imagine myself present at the last meal of Jesus with his close friends. The apostles are puzzled, and Jesus is sad and troubled by his approaching death; he is concerned about giving his apostles an important experience to remember. As I listen to Peter's question and his insistence that Jesus will never wash his feet, I wonder how I would react. Although washing feet is not our custom, even if I had lived at that time I would have felt uncomfortable with the idea of the Lord washing my feet. I would have resisted as Peter did. Jesus is so insistent with Peter, "If I do not wash you, you can have nothing in common with me." This language is so strong. If Peter continues to refuse, he will cut himself off completely from Jesus and his ministry. The outlook of Jesus is that the master and servant wash each other's feet; one is not to dominate the other. In Jesus' community, everyone is equal; everyone is bound by service and love. Peter, the leader, needs to understand that message if he is to share in Jesus' life and ministry. How far we have wandered from this ideal. I am so much a part of a domination system; I don't like to be served because it makes me feel weak. Sometimes I consider myself superior to others. I need to learn the same thing Jesus is insisting that Peter learn. It's hard in my life and in my society to fight categorizing people, to live according to Jesus' notion of love and equality, but I have no choice if I am to have a share in my life and ministry. Jesus asks if they understand what he has done to them. I hope I understand. If Jesus, Master and Lord, washed their feet, they should wash one another's. This kind of service to others is to be the mark of the Christian community, the expression of our love for one another in Christ Jesus. The kind of service that always puts another's needs ahead of my own is difficult, but Jesus promises happiness to those who love and serve as he loved and served. I cannot claim a close relationship with Jesus, his Father and his Spirit in prayer and not follow his commands and live as he lived—in a life of love. To put on Christ is to let his vision, his heart, his love become mine, and part of doing this is expressed in this Gospel. Loving service without domination is what Jesus commands and what I must, with his help, try to live.

Lord Jesus, I feel challenged by this Gospel reading. I need your help and your strength to serve and to love the way you are insisting that Peter and the apostles do. I trust that you are with me as I try to live as a Christian. The more I come to know you through your word and your presence, the more confident I become that I can live your life-style of love even in this crazy world of ours. I trust the promise you have made to be with me all days, and I count on you to continue your faithful loving and caring all the days of my life.

Amen.

Other references:
Matthew 16:13–20 Peter's Profession of Faith
John 21:15–19 Peter, Do You Love Me?

Bibliography

Barbotin, Edward. *Faith for Today.* Maryknoll: Orbis Books, 1974.
Donovan. *Christianity Rediscovered.* Notre Dame: Fides/Claretian, 1978.
Fowler, James and Sam Keen. *Life Maps: Conversations on the Journey of Faith.* Waco: Word, 1978.
Greeley, Andrew. *May the Wind Be at Your Back.* New York: Seabury Press, 1975.
Merton, Thomas. *He Is Risen.* Niles: Argus Communications, 1975.
Nolan, Albert. *Jesus Before Christianity.* New York: Orbis Books, 1978.
Nouwen, Henri. *The Living Reminder.* New York: Seabury Press, 1977.
O'Shea, Kevin. *The Way of Tenderness.* New York: Paulist Press, 1978.
Peoples Mass Book. Cincinnati: World Library of Sacred Music, 1970.
Powell, John, S.J. *Fully Human, Fully Alive.* Niles: Argus Communications, 1976.
Sanford, John. *Healing and Wholeness.* New York: Paulist Press, 1977.

Chapter 6

Faith Connections

Flashback

You can become more aware of your faith-development by using your imagination and memory. Look at the pictures at the beginning of this chapter. Examine each picture carefully to see whether it triggers any memories for you. Relax and let your imagination work. As you study the picture of the sunset, you may recall a time when you had a pleasant visit with a friend or relative. As you look at the rose, you may recall a special relationship, or perhaps a sad experience. Some memories may be happy; others may be sad. No picture will trigger the same memory in any two people. This exercise is a way to help you to be more conscious of your own faith-life and to see the connection between everyday experience and faith.

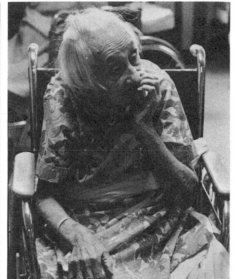

After you have spent some time reflecting on the pictures, choose five that meant something special to you. Write the image in the column marked "Visual." Write the event that was triggered in your memory and then describe the significance of the event.

Some Examples	Visual	Event	Significance
	Rose	Senior prom	I realized in a new way that I was special to someone
	Rose	My father's death	I experienced a great loss and separation

Flashback Experience

Visual	Event	Significance
1.		
2.		

Flashback Experience

	Visual	Event	Significance
3.			
4.			
5.			

For Reflection

Frequently, the major significance of events is not understood until sometime after their occurrence. You may become conscious of the faith-element of an event only by reflecting on it at a later date. Choose three events from the list you have made and think about how they relate to your faith-life. Write about them in your journal.

Prayer. Express in the form of a prayer the feelings, needs, desires, and hopes that this experience of remembering has stirred in you.

Making Connections with Jesus' Life

Making Connections with Jesus' Life is an exercise to help you see a relationship between your life and the life of Jesus. The awareness of such a relationship is an aid to the development of faith.

Jesus spent much of his time doing many of the same things you do in your everyday life. There is an advantage to reflecting on how you are like Jesus, rather than the usual approach of reflecting on how Jesus is so different from us. In the Gospels, we read that Jesus frequently used his hands to change people's lives. We also use our hands, our talents and abilities, to make a difference in people's lives and to change the world. Use the following exercise to make connections between your life and the life of Jesus.

Scripture	How did Jesus Use His Hands? What did He do with His Hands?	How do I Use My Hands in Ways Reminiscent of Jesus?
Matthew 14:31 "Jesus put out his hand at once and held him."	Example: Jesus was supportive.	I held out my hands as I helped my children to walk. I embraced my neighbor as she told me of her mother's death.
Mark 1:31 "He went to her, took her by the hand and helped her up."		
Luke 7:13–15 "When the Lord saw her he felt sorry for her. 'Do not cry,' he said. Then he went up and put his hand on the bier . . . and said 'Young man, I tell you to get up.' "		
Luke 8:54–55 "But taking her by the hand he called to her, 'Child, get up.' "		
Luke 9:16 "He took the five loaves and two fish . . . said the blessing . . . then he broke them and handed them to his disciples."		
Luke 9:47–48 "He took a little child and set him by his side."		
John 13:5 "Taking a towel, (he) wrapped it around his waist; he then poured water into a basin and began to wash the disciples' feet and to wipe them with the towel."		

Scripture	How did Jesus Use His Hands? What did He do with His Hands?	How do I Use My Hands in Ways Reminiscent of Jesus?
John 21:9–21 "As soon as they came ashore they saw that there was some bread there, and a charcoal fire with fish cooking on it. Jesus said, 'Bring some of the fish you have just caught. . . .' " (read the entire passage)		
Matthew 9:29 "He touched their eyes saying, 'Your faith deserves it.' "		
John 9:6–7 "Having said this, he spat on the ground, made a paste . . . (and) put it over the eyes of the blind man."		

Praying for Wholeness

Use the following for private or group reflection. If used for group participation, follow the notations in the left-hand margin. If used privately, disregard the notations.

Introduction

The "life-force within us" is the shared life of God, in both human and spiritual terms. Prayer is a communication; it is an attempt to deepen our friendship with the God who has shared life with us. Through prayer, we begin to reach toward the center of our being and through this "restlessness of search" begin to find the holiness that is wholeness.

If this is used for group participation, begin with an opening hymn.

Part I

Leader Prayer is a personal response to a call, to the law. It is not written on stone but in our hearts.

Side A "Our hearts are restless until they rest in you, O Lord" (St. Augustine).

Side B "Deep within them I will plant my law, writing it on their hearts. Then I will be their God and they shall be my people" (Jeremiah 31:33).

Side A "There came a mighty wind . . . but Yahweh was not in the wind. After the wind came an earthquake. But Yahweh was not in the earthquake. After the earthquake came a fire. But Yahweh was not in the fire. After the fire there came the sound of a gentle breeze. . . . Then a voice came to him" (1 Kings 19:11–14).

Together "When we cannot choose words in order to pray properly, the Spirit himself expresses our plea in a way that could never be put into words, and God who knows everything in our hearts knows perfectly well what he means, and that the pleas of the saints expressed by the Spirit are according to the mind of God" (Romans 8:26–27).

All Silent prayer.

Part II

Leader Prayer is a means to our personal conversion to the Lord. God's holy word challenges us, supports us, awakens us to change our ways—to rid ourselves of the selfishness and callousness of which we are capable.

Side A The Lord Yahweh says: "I shall give you a new heart, and put a new spirit in you; I shall remove the heart of stone from your bodies and give you a heart of flesh instead" (Ezekiel 36:26).

Side B "Israel, come back to Yahweh your God; your iniquity was the cause of your downfall. Provide yourself with words and come back to Yahweh" (Hosea 14:2–3).

Together "So then, if you are bringing your offering to the altar and there remember that your brother has something against you, leave your offering there before the altar, and go and be reconciled first, and then come back and present your offering" (Matthew 5:23–24).

All Silent Prayer.

Part III

Leader Prayer is a path to living out the Gospel. Prayer cannot be a passive activity carried out in isolation. Rather, like Jesus, we seek silence and quiet in order to return renewed, richer in faith, hope, and charity.

Side A "Peace I bequeath to you, my own peace I give you" (John 14:27).
"Peace is simply the restlessness of search" (Thomas Francoer).

Side B "To live is to change; to be perfect is to have changed often!" (John Henry Newman).

Side A "The glory of God is man fully alive!" (Saint Irenaeus).

Side B "The one who infringes even one of the least of these commandments and teaches others to do the same will be considered the least in the kingdom of heaven; but the man who keeps them and teaches them will be considered great in the kingdom of heaven" (Matthew 5:19).

Together "Be compassionate as your Father is compassionate. Do not judge, and you will not be judged yourselves; do not condemn, and you will not be condemned yourselves; grant pardon, and you will be pardoned. Give, and there will be gifts for you: a full measure, pressed down, shaken together, and running over, will be poured into your lap; because the amount you measure out is the amount you will be given back" (Luke 6:36–38).

All Silent prayer.

Prayer and Unity

Prayer helps us bring unity to our lives. Through prayer we try to integrate all the facets and dimensions of our lives into a deeper consciousness of who we are. When one of the Pharisees asked, "Which is the greatest commandment of the law?" Jesus replied, "You must love the Lord your God with all your heart, with all your soul, and with all your mind. This is the greatest and the first commandment. The second resembles it: You must love your neighbor as yourself" (Matthew 22:35–39). Jesus' reply includes the command to pray, to lift our minds and hearts to our Creator, and to serve those created in his image.

Thomas Francoer, a psychologist, has said, "Peace is simply the restlessness of search." That also tells us something about prayer. Prayer is the kind of activity that Jesus spoke about when he described the greatest commandments. St. Gregory of Nyssa once declared: "The soul who is troubled is near unto God." The Swiss psychiatrist C.G. Jung emphasized our need to strive toward wholeness, calling this process of personality development *individuation.* In his book *Healing and Wholeness,* author John Sanford describes the process this way:

> "Wholeness calls for the fulfillment of our potentiality, but this can never be achieved, for human potentiality is too rich, and the demands of life upon us are constantly changing and calling forth new responses. The whole person is an *ideal* that can never be realized. Nevertheless, what it means for us to be whole seems to be known in the unconscious center of our being, and it is from this center that the process of individuation is begun. We do not 'decide' to become whole; rather, it is thrust upon us by the life force within us."

Striving for Wholeness

According to an old saying, there are times when we "can't see the forest for the trees." This happens when we focus on and compartmentalize parts of our lives and then fail to see how they fit together. This happens, for example, when people let one bad experience destroy their sense of humor or self-confidence.

Striving for the "center," the holiness and wholeness of one's life, the "real me," requires a consciousness of and response to three aspects, or segments, of life. The accompanying diagram is meant to demonstrate how these three dimensions intersect and interrelate. Faith-development, the core of the diagram, becomes the key and the resulting aspect with which we should be concerned.

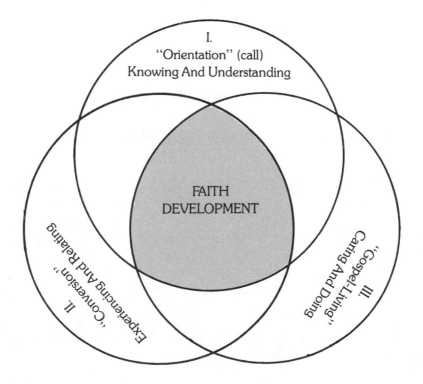

You might ask yourself the following questions in order to become more aware of your faith-development.

- What has changed in each of these areas that enables me to experience a deeper and more balanced faith-development?
- Is my faith one-sided or two-sided? Does my prayer-life lead to witness, service, and worship with the community? How is faith related to justice, to the arms race?
- What is lacking, what is needed for a proper balance of faith-development in my life?
- How can I improve each of these aspects in order to have them touch my faith-development in a balanced way?

Use the following for reflection on your faith life:

- "I have already succeeded in . . ."
- "I would like to . . ."
- "I need to . . ."
- "I hope to . . ."
- "I should . . ."
- "I want . . ."
- "I could . . ."
- "I can . . ."
- "I will begin to . . ."

Scriptural Reflections

Refer to Chapter 4 for specific suggestions about ways to pray with Scripture.

Holy Ground

God's presence is found on "a holy ground." "Holy ground" is everywhere around us. Ground becomes holy when we recognize the presence of God in it. Reflect upon places that are holy ground for you. Are there any special areas of your home where you have been especially aware of God's presence? Where are the special areas apart from home where you have recognized God's presence? How does recognizing God's presence contribute to the sense of unity in life? How does recognizing the presence of God affect faith?

Use the following Scripture passages to reflect upon the trust God has in us to make his presence known.

Exodus 3:4–5	Romans 8:28–31	1 Corinthians 4:1–5
Isaiah 42:1–6	Matthew 5:13–16	

Intimacy with the Lord

In order that faith can grow, we need to recognize God's desire to be one with us and respond to the call of God. Use the following passages to reflect on God's desire for intimacy. How does a sense of intimacy with God contribute to our wholeness?

Jeremiah 13:1–11   Romans 8:1–13   Acts 17:28
John 3:13   John 5:4–12

Bibliography

Kelsey, Morton T. *Caring.* New York: Paulist Press, 1981.
Mackey, James P. *Jesus, the Man and the Myth.* New York: Paulist Press, 1979.
Westley, Richard. *Redemptive Intimacy.* Mystic: Twenty-Third Publications, 1981.

Chapter 7

Spiritual Life as a Journey

The Pilgrimage of the Church

In this chapter, we will look at the spiritual life as a journey. We are the people of God on pilgrimage; each of us is on a journey toward the heavenly Jerusalem. It is a journey that calls for heroism. God offers his Son as the way and his Spirit as the source of strength and love on the journey. In the following excerpts from *The Constitution on the Church* (Vatican II), it is clear that the entire Church is on a journey toward the kingdom of God.

> "All human persons are called to this union with Christ, who is the light of the world, from whom we go forth, through whom we live, and toward whom our journey leads us" (paragraph 3).
> "Still in pilgrimage upon the earth, we trace in trial and under oppression the paths he trod. Made one with his sufferings as the body is one with the head, we endure with him, that with him we may be glorified" (paragraph 7).
> "For even now on this earth the Church is marked with a genuine though imperfect holiness. However, until there is a new heaven and a new earth where justice dwells (cf. 2 Peter 3:13), the pilgrim Church in its sacraments and institutions, which pertain to this present time, takes on the appearance of this passing world. It itself dwells among creatures who groan and travail in pain until now and await the revelation of the sons of God" (paragraph 48).

Spend at least five minutes meditating on these passages from *The Documents of Vatican II*.

Jesus' Journey to Jerusalem

Seeing that the Church considers itself a holy people on pilgrimage, it should come as no surprise that this concept, or image, has been taken from the Old Testament and is deeply rooted in the very life or journey of Jesus.

Prayer was a significant part of Jesus' life. Through prayer he realized his mission and received strength for his life's journey. He often went into the hills and would spend the whole night in prayer. Jesus prays "alone in the presence of his disciples" and later goes "up a mountain to pray." Jesus is changed through prayer. He came to greater self-understanding through prayer. He became aware of his mission through prayer.

Even though he was a man of prayer, he was still very active. He was a man on the move—teaching, healing, consoling, feeding the hungry, doing justice, and righting the wrongs around him. He was willing to lay down his life so that a new life might begin. Jesus' love was an attempt to die, in the sense that he was ready to "burn out" in order to break through the confinement and limitations he himself experienced in his working and waking hours. He understood that much of what is promised us takes place on the other side of death and therefore to hinder that death was self-defeating.

In a little book entitled *Archy and Mehitabel* by Don Marquis, there is an episode entitled "The Lesson of the Moth." It relates the story of a moth that flutters around and around, constantly darting into a candle's flame, attracted by its brilliance. Finally, the moth accomplishes what it set out to do—it burns itself up in an instant. The writer concludes: "At the same time I wish there was something I wanted as badly as he wanted to fry himself."

Where did Jesus get this burning desire to "set his face steadfastly toward Jerusalem"? Luke's Gospel makes it quite plain by setting that statement *in the midst* of Jesus' prayer life. Jesus took time to pray, to evaluate himself, to become so finely attuned to his Father that he could *trust* that God's presence and power would be with him at *every* step of his life's journey.

For Reflection

1. How would you summarize Jesus' mission in one or two sentences?
2. How did Jesus grow in knowledge of his mission through prayer? Cite examples.
3. Luke states that Jesus prayed "alone in the presence of his disciples" (Luke 9:18). What do you think this means?
4. Jesus' prayer opened him up not only to his Father but to other people. He did not use prayer as an escape from the sufferings of the world. What were some of the ways he showed concern for others? Can you see connections between your prayer life and your concern for some of the same issues Jesus was concerned about? Explain.
5. What is the point of the moth story for you?
6. Think about some goals you have set in your life, something you want very badly. If you wish, share this with your group or a friend. Are any of your goals similar to Jesus' goals?
7. Read Luke, Chapters 6, 9, 10, and 11, for further insights into Jesus' prayer-life.

Journey in Faith

Use the following pictures for reflection. You may wish to write your thoughts in your journal.

1. Road
Each of us is on a journey toward the kingdom. Like pilgrims in search, we are on a long and winding road, but our search has a definite end: our destiny is union with God. The movement of our spiritual journeys is always a movement of owning and accepting our humanness.

Describe the road you have followed in your faith-journey. Has your road been smooth or bumpy? Have you encountered dead ends or new horizons? How does the road ahead look? Who is with you as you travel?

2. Stop Sign

A stop sign on our spiritual journey is an event or experience that brings us to a sudden halt, and eventually to a new discovery. It might be awareness of sin, sickness, failure, falling in love, death, or a new beginning. Experiences such as these can often turn our lives around; through deep sadness or great joy, we can discover something new about God, ourselves, or our world.

What stop signs come immediately to mind? How did you feel about each event as it happened? How do you feel now? Where was God when the "stop sign" entered your life?

3. Rest Area or Wayside

The rest areas or waysides can be times of solitude, nourishment, or fun. They give us encouragement and energy for the journey. Jesus said, "Come to me, all you who labor and are overburdened, and I will give you rest" (Matthew 11:28).

Do you have time to be alone, a place where you can rest and pray?

Are you able to quiet down sufficiently so that you can listen to your life?

4. Mountaintop

Mountaintop experiences are times of peace and fulfillment. They are occasions when we get an overview of life, a deep feeling that life is good and that we are glad to be a part of it. They bring a touch of glory, because we know that we are loved by God or by another person; because we have seen a wonder of nature and are moved by it; because we witness the miracle of birth, or a change of heart by someone we love or are praying for. Mountaintop experiences can come into sight anywhere along the road; they affect us for a lifetime.

Can you recall your last mountaintop experience? What were your feelings? What did it do to your life?

5. Intersection

"Two roads diverged in a wood, and I—
I took the one less traveled by,
And that has made all the difference."
Robert Frost
The Road Not Taken

You could have worked for one company but you chose another; you could have entered religious life but you married; you could have lived in another part of the country but you chose this one; you could have abandoned a particular relationship but you got involved. Decisions such as these are the intersections of your journey. They have given you insights and have greatly influenced the direction of your life.

Have you accepted the road taken at important intersections of your life?
How have people affected your decision to take one road rather than another?

How do you feel about those people and your choices? How have you extended yourself to help others on their journey? Listen to the Spirit in your heart; he will help you to recognize the ways you are being called to share your life with others at this time.

Jesus, A Busy Person, A Person on a Journey

Reflect on the following passages from the Gospel of Mark. In each one of them, we see Jesus as a busy person on a journey who needed time and made time for prayer.

Mark 1:14–18

"After John had been arrested, Jesus went into Galilee. There he proclaimed the Good News from God. 'The time has come,' he said, 'and the kingdom of God is close at hand. Repent, and believe the Good News.'

"As he was walking along by the Sea of Galilee he saw Simon and his brother Andrew casting a net in the lake—for they were fishermen. And Jesus said to them, 'Follow me and I will make you fishers of men.' And at once they left their nets and followed him."

Mark 1:21

"They went as far as Capernaum, and as soon as the sabbath came he went to the synagogue and began to teach."

Mark 1:29–31

"On leaving the synagogue, he went with James and John straight to the house of Simon and Andrew. Now Simon's mother-in-law had gone to bed with fever, and they told him about her straightaway. He went to her, took her by the hand and helped her up. And the fever left her and she began to wait on them."

Mark 1:35

"In the morning, long before dawn, he got up and left the house, and went off to a lonely place and prayed there."

Mark 2:13

"He went out again to the shore of the lake; and all the people came to him, and he taught them."

Mark 3:7–8

"Jesus withdrew with his disciples to the lakeside, and great crowds from Galilee followed him. From Judaea, Jerusalem, Idumaea, Transjordania and the region of Tyre and Sidon, great numbers who had heard of all he was doing came to him."

Mark 3:20

"He went home again and once more such a crowd collected that they could not even have a meal."

Mark 6:1

"Going from that district, he went to his home town and his disciples accompanied him."

Mark 7:24

"He left that place and set out for the territory of Tyre. There he went into a house and did not want anyone to know he was there, but he could not pass unrecognized."

Mark 9:33

"They came to Capernaum, and when he was in the house he asked them, 'What were you arguing about on the road?'"

Mark 14:12

"On the first day of Unleavened Bread, when the Passover lamb was sacrificed, his disciples said to him, 'Where do you want us to go and make the preparations for you to eat the Passover?'"

For Reflection

1. Can you relate to the busyness of Jesus? How did he find time to pray? Where in your busy life can you find time to pray?
2. Can you pray when you are with people? In your car? Working in the kitchen or garage?
3. Have you read about people or have you read the writings of people known to be extremely busy but also deeply prayerful? Consider the following individuals:
   - Mother Teresa
   - Pope John Paul II
   - Thomas Merton
   - Dorothy Day
   - Catherine de Hueck
   - St. Frances Cabrini
   - St. Vincent de Paul
   - St. Elizabeth (Mother) Seton

Inquire at your local library to learn more about these people and how they managed to pray and still be concerned about many things. Consider *The Classics of Western Spirituality* (Paulist Press) as a source for reading about people who were deeply involved in life but still had time to pray.

Meditations About Journeying

The following references are for your prayer. Imagine yourself present in these situations and on a journey with Jesus. What questions would you ask him? Are these parts of his journey in any way connected with your own journey?

Luke 24:13–35   The Road to Emmaus
Luke 9:51–62   The Journey to Jerusalem
Mark 9:2–8   The Transfiguration

Reflect on the following quotations. They are taken from *Journeys,* a book edited by Gregory Baum.

"As Hitler tore asunder the web of our life, nothing remained of the ideals that inspired us. When, as a boy of sixteen, I was able to leave Germany for England in 1939, I felt that my world had gone under. The people I knew, my family and friends had become mute. They had nothing to say. None of the inherited values shed light on the new situation. Life had lost all meaning. I well remember how amazed I was at the silence of my elders. It was soon afterward that I began to search for a view of life and a source of wisdom that could outlast catastrophe. In Canada, in 1946, I became a Christian in the Catholic Church.

"In him (Jesus Christ), we discover what human life is about. Christ reveals to us the grace operative in every human being. What Christian believers encounter in Christ is, therefore, their own depth. They discover in Christ the mystery at work in their lives from the beginning, and because they are now able to name it, they are able to relate themselves more consciously to it and thus reorient their own personal history. Jesus Christ is unique because he raises man's consciousness about what really goes on in their lives and thereby initiates them into a new relationship to one another and to the divine ground out of which they came to be."

Gregory Baum

"My own mandala began to become visible to me in those classes, and ever since then I have seen mandalas emerging, diverging, converging in people's lives and in various traditions. People's life experiences change, drastic things happen, disasters threaten or strike but the mandalas do not break. They transcend all this because they are the cumulative vision and wisdom of many generations."

Monika Hellwig

"To understand the religious a person need not travel around the world, speak a dozen languages, and have read the literature of East and West. One needs only to have experienced the ordinary in unordinary ways. This principle is not an anti-intellectual one because it has been arrived at by, among others, people who have made intellectual journeys. Religious inquiry pushed to the limits brings us back home again to the simplicities of our beginning."

Gabriel Moran

For Reflection
1. With which of the above can you best identify?
2. Reflect on your journey in terms of major movements. Where have you been? Where are you going? How does your journey resemble the journey of Jesus? Use your journal to write your reflections.

Bibliography

Abbott, Walter M., S.J., ed. *Documents of Vatican II.* New York: Guild, 1966.

Baum, Gregory. *Journeys.* New York: Paulist Press, 1975.

Hauser, Richard, S.J. *In His Spirit: A Guide to Today's Spirituality.* New York: Paulist Press, 1982.

Hellman, Lillian. *Pentimento.* New York: Signet Books, 1973.

Hesse, Hermann. *Siddhartha.* New York: Bantam Books, 1951.

Lane, Dermot. *The Reality of Jesus.* New York: Paulist Press, 1975.

Marquis, Don. *Archy and Mehitabel.* Garden City: Doubleday, 1930.

Novak, Michael. *Ascent of the Mountain, Flight of the Dove.* New York: Harper and Row, 1971.

Payne, Richard J. ed., *The Classics of Western Spirituality.* New York: Paulist Press, 1978–1983.

Powell, John, S.J. *He Touched Me.* Niles: Argus Communications, 1974.

Sanford, John A. *The Man Who Wrestled with God.* New York: Paulist Press, 1974.

Whitehead, Evelyn and James. *Christian Life Patterns.* Garden City: Doubleday, 1979.

Chapter 8

Listening and Seeing

Listening and Seeing

To be a Christian is to see the extraordinary in the ordinary, to see beyond the everyday routine, to see more than meets the eye. The following passages can help us reflect on what is beyond the ordinary in everyday life experiences.

Saint Joan
In this scene from *Saint Joan,* a play by Bernard Shaw, King Charles asks Joan of Arc why she always seems to know what is best to do.

Joan:	"I always know. My voices—
King Charles:	Oh your voices, your voices. Why dont the voices come to me. I am king, not you."
Joan:	They do come to you; but you do not hear them. You have not sat in the field in the evening listening for them. When the angelus rings you cross yourself and have done with it; but if you prayed from your heart, and listened to the trilling of the bells in the air after they stop ringing, you would hear the voices as well as I do."

St. Francis of Assisi

Francis of Assisi faced oppression, struggle and failure. When he reflected on the dark side of life, however, he found an extraordinary song of joy threading its way through life.

Prayer of St. Francis

Lord, make me an instrument of your peace;
where there is hatred, let me sow love;
where there is injury, pardon;
where there is doubt, faith;
where there is despair, hope;
where there is darkness, light;
and where there is sadness, joy.
Grant that I may not so much seek to be consoled as to console;
to be understood, as to understand,
to be loved, as to love;
for it is in giving that we receive,
it is in pardoning that we are pardoned,
and it is in dying that we are born to eternal life.

Mother Teresa

People such as Dr. Tom Dooley, Dorothy Day, and Mother Teresa have found God in the wretched poor and suffering persons throughout the world. The following is a paraphrase of a statement made by Mother Teresa:

> People ask me: "Why do you waste your time bringing these dying beggars off the street and into your clinic to bathe their wounds and care for them? They're going to die anyway!" And I answer, "Yes, but these people have never seen anything beautiful or been loved—and just once, before they die, we must demonstrate to them that they are good and worthwhile and that we care about them!"

Godspell

In the early 1970s, a young man left the Easter Vigil service in his Church because it had been so boring, hurried, and matter-of-fact. He returned home and wrote a play that for him embodied the celebration of life. The name of the play was *Godspell,* and it became a box-office success on stage and screen. What was the man seeing that prompted him to create *Godspell?*

Bernstein

When conductor Leonard Bernstein was commissioned to write something for the opening of the Kennedy Center for the Performing Arts in Washington, D.C. in 1971, this renowned Jewish composer chose the Roman Catholic Mass, as a living reminder of God's presence and Word. In the paraphrase below he explains why.

"I was fascinated with this ritual and its symbolic value to affirm my concern that the principal crisis of this century is a crisis of faith." And why? Because of our inability *to see* and *hear deeply* the mystery of God in our lives.

Exodus

Read Exodus 3:1–12. Then reflect on the following excerpt from *Aurora Leigh* by Elizabeth Barrett Browning.

> "Earth's crammed with heaven,
> and every common bush
> afire with God;
> But only he who sees,
> takes off his shoes—
> The rest sit around it
> and pluck blackberries."

Serenity Prayer

The Serenity Prayer is one that is prayed throughout the world by recovering alcoholics, drug addicts and others as they struggle with their daily problems.

> "God grant me the grace to accept the things I cannot change;
> the strength to change the things I can;
> and the wisdom to know the difference."

Select one of these passages that is especially meaningful to you. How do you identify with it? How is the extraordinary seen in the ordinary? Reread the passage slowly and use it for ten minutes of personal prayer.

Listening and Seeing Anew
A Photo Meditation

A Christian is a person who sees more than meets the eye. The following reflection may help us be more sensitive to the beauty and meaning found in daily life.

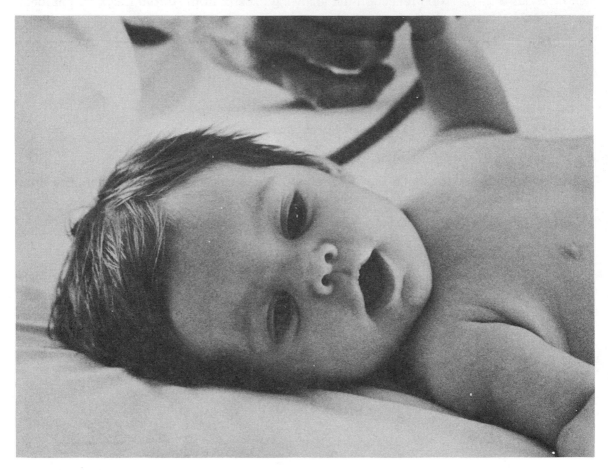

A. What do you see?
A newborn infant.

B. What do you *see*?
- The result of two people's love for each other.
- The answer to some woman's long and faithful prayer for a child.
- The possibility of a great artist or statesperson at prayer.
- A "pearl of great price" who almost didn't make it into this world but who lives among us because of a miracle of modern medicine.

C. What do *you* see?

A. What do you see?
Fresh flowing water.

B. What do you *see*?
- A source of life for fish and plants.
- A source of power for a city.
- A cause of someone's reflection on the flow and movement of one's life.
- A symbol of life's journey over rocks and around curves, but with a strong sense of direction.

C. What do *you* see?

A. What do you see?
A city.

B. What do you *see*?
- Intensity of living: fast-paced, mysterious, full of life and a multitude of stories.
- An invitation to crime.
- Big business, competition, a cut-throat lifestyle in which it is tough to survive.
- Center for art, inspiration for many, culture for the masses. Underdeveloped model of the new Church, the new Jerusalem awaiting a creative hand and word.

C. What do *you* see?

A. What do you *see*?
An elderly person.

B. What do you *see*?
- The wisdom of the ages in the eyes of this person.
- A victim of our harsh, youth-oriented society.
- A grandparent who gives life anew to young children.
- A "faithful servant" in the last phase of the journey to eternal freedom.

C. What do *you* see?

A. What do you see?
Fire.

B. What do you *see*?
  • A symbol of the intensity, color, movement, power of God.
  • A good time, a marvelous fall evening, a homecoming victory.
  • A burning bush: the one Moses saw, Israel as burning bush, Martin Luther King as burning bush, Jesus as burning bush; burning up with love and zeal, but never being destroyed.

C. What do *you* see?

A. What do you see?

A wedding.

B. What do you *see?*

- The beginning of life together, of growth in life, of experience in intimacy.
- A symbol of the closeness of Jesus Christ with his Church.
- A challenge to faithfulness; a journey toward maturity together.
- The culmination of a romance begun in childhood; the time of commitment even unto death.

C. What do *you* see?

A. What do you see?
A football game.

B. What do you *see*?
- The great American "liturgical" celebration.
- An acting out of man's inhumanity to man.
- Recreation supreme; a very good time.
- The focus of competition and money and power.
- The thing that makes Saturday/Sunday "sacred" in the United States.

C. What do *you* see?

A. What do you see?

A cemetery.

B. What do you *see*?

- Separation from a loving parent and grief not yet lived through.
- The end of the journey and celebration forever.
- A thousand fears and a strong denial.
- Peace at last after endless struggle.

C. What do *you* see?

The Notion of Surprise

At the Last Supper, Jesus got up from the table, set aside his garments, put on an apron and deliberately (and dramatically) began to wash his disciples' feet. In reality, as the host of this Jewish ritual dinner for Passover, this was the *common* and expected thing for him to do. Read the following New Testament passages and the reflections on them. Jesus made the expected into the unexpected, the commonplace into the special, the unusual into the usual, the ordinary into the extraordinary. Notice in the passages that follow how Jesus effects a surprising turn of events.

John 13:1–16

"Jesus knew that the Father had put everything into his hands, and that he had come from God and was returning to God, and he got up from table, removed his outer garment and, taking a towel, wrapped it round his waist; he then poured water into a basin and began to wash the disciples' feet and to wipe them with the towel he was wearing.

He came to Simon Peter, who said to him, 'Lord, are you going to wash my feet?' Jesus answered, 'At the moment you do not know what I am doing, but later you will understand.' 'Never!' said Peter 'You shall never wash my feet.' Jesus replied, 'If I do not wash you, you can have nothing in common with me.' 'Then, Lord,' said Simon Peter 'not only my feet, but my hands and my head as well!' Jesus said, 'No one who has taken a bath needs washing, he is clean all over. You too are clean, though not all of you are.' He knew who was going to betray him, that was why he said, 'though not all of you are.'

When he had washed their feet and put on his clothes again he went back to the table. 'Do you understand' he said 'what I have done to you? You call me Master and Lord, and rightly; so I am. If I, then, the Lord and Master, have washed your feet, you should wash each other's feet. I have given you an example so that you may copy what I have done to you.''

Luke 12:35–40

"See that you are dressed for action and have your lamps lit. Be like men waiting for their master to return from the wedding feast, ready to open the door as soon as he comes and knocks. Happy those servants whom the master finds awake when he comes. I tell you solemnly, he will put on an apron, sit them down at table and wait on them. It may be in the second watch he comes, or in the third, but happy those servants if he finds them ready. You may be quite sure of this, that if the householder had known at what hour the burglar would come, he would not have let anyone break through the wall of his house. You too must stand ready.''

Luke 10:1–10

"After this the Lord appointed seventy-two others and sent them out ahead of him, in pairs, to all the towns and places he himself was to visit. He said to them, 'The harvest is rich but the laborers are few, so ask the Lord of the harvest to send laborers to his harvest. Start off now, but remember, I am sending you out like lambs among wolves. Carry no purse, no haversack, no sandals. Salute no one on the road. Whatever house you go into, let your first words be, 'Peace to this house!' And if a man of peace lives there, your peace will go and rest on him; if not, it will come back to you. Stay in the same house, taking what food and drink they have to offer, for the laborer deserves his wages; do not move from house to house. Whenever you go into a town where they make you welcome, eat what is set before you. Cure those in it who are sick, and say, 'The kingdom of God is very near to you.' ''

Luke 10:17–20

''The seventy-two came back rejoicing. 'Lord,' they said, 'even the devils submit to us when we use your name.' He said to them, 'I watched Satan fall like lightning from heaven. Yes, I have given you power to tread underfoot serpents and scorpions and the whole strength of the enemy; nothing shall ever hurt you. You do not rejoice that the spirits submit to you; rejoice rather that your names are written in heaven.' ''

More Reflections

Over and over, the Gospels are full of surprises. For those who see deeply and listen carefully, there is much more than meets the eye. The commonplace becomes special, and the ordinary becomes extraordinary because what is essential is often invisible to the eye.

What turn of events causes surprise in the above passages?

The next time you read the Gospels, watch for the element of surprise. Discover the extraordinary in the ordinary.

Reflections on Listening and Seeing

I. Read the following Scripture passages aloud with a friend, if possible. Reflect together on the passages and think about the questions related to seeing and listening.

John 9:1–38

- Why did the Pharisees refuse to listen when the blind man told his story?
- Are there stories or people you refuse to listen to? Think about them.
- What did the blind man ''see'' that the Pharisees did not see?
- What events or persons in your life have helped you to see more than meets the eye?

John 14:1–11

- Jesus says, ''I am the way, the truth and the life.'' What do you ''see'' in this statement?
- Why did some people see Jesus as a carpenter only, and others as the way, the truth and the life?
- What did Jesus mean when he said, ''To have seen me is to have seen the Father''? What special kind of seeing does this take?
- Can you recall some ordinary or extraordinary events in your life that revealed God's life or presence to you?
- Why do you think so many saw and heard Jesus, but so few actually followed him?

II. Sacred Space

Make a list of sacred space in your life—that is, persons, places, moments where you think God has touched you in a special way. What ordinary moments have been cherished as "extraordinary"—as moments of prayer?

What was your special moment?	What was your prayer when you experienced that event? Were you aware of the event as related to prayer?	What is your prayer now as you look back on that special moment?
Persons		
Nature		
Books		
Poetry		
Memories		
TV, Movies		
Experiences		
Religious Experiences		

Make a sketch or blueprint of your home and mark the areas where you have encountered God. Describe them. What was your prayer at these moments? Where do you find prayer? When do you need prayer? How is prayer related to each of the following words?

loneliness	play	hope
love	work	joy
sacrifice	laughter	discouragement
sickness	beauty	justice

III. Try to do the following reflection with one other person. Consider each of the stories below. After each statement, talk about the struggles, events and feelings involved in the accomplishment stated. Create the middle part of the story. Use your imagination and talk about what parts of the statement involve more than meets the eye. Jot down some of your insights.

A. A three-year-old child takes her first step and everyone in the family cheers for her.
Fact: This child was born with a hole in her spine.
Comments:

B. Jim had a party to celebrate his promotion to vice-president of his company after five years of outstanding work for the firm.
Fact: Jim was a severe alcoholic ten years ago. He could not hold a job, and his marriage almost dissolved.
Comments:

C. A young couple who had a combined income of $30,000 a year now have an income of only $17,000. They have one child and are a very happy and committed couple.

Fact: The couple made a decision to simplify their lives and to give up their own business, taking lower-paying, less pressured, and less prestigious jobs.

Comments:

Bibliography

Berrigan, Daniel. *Portraits of Those I Love.* New York: Crossroad, 1982.

Fischer, Kathleen R. *The Inner Rainbow.* New York: Paulist Press, 1983.

Holmes, Urban T., III. *Ministry and Imagination.* New York: Seabury Press, 1976.

Kelsey, Morton. *Caring.* New York: Paulist Press, 1981.

Muggeridge, Malcolm. *Something Beautiful for God: Mother Teresa of Calcutta.* Garden City: Doubleday, 1977.

Paton, Alan, and Ray Ellis. *Instrument of Thy Peace.* New York: Seabury Press, 1975.

Raines, Robert. *Lord, Could You Make It A Little Better?* Waco: Word Books, 1976.

Sanford, John A. *Healing and Wholeness.* New York: Paulist Press, 1977.

Shaw, George Bernard. "Saint Joan," *Collected Plays.* New York: Dodd Mead & Co., 1970.

Chapter 9

Sin and Forgiveness

Part I—The Reality of Sin and Forgiveness

Sin does exist; it is real. It exists in each of us, in our small communities, and throughout the world. Although sin has some strange role to play in the redemption of each one of us, and in the world, it is not greater than God. Mysteriously, God permits sin, but certainly God can and will heal us of sin. Although there is no such thing as a person without sin, there are many people who have no consciousness of personal, community or social sin.

There are many ways of explaining sin. According to author John Shea, "sin is forgetfulness of creaturehood." It is denying dependence on God, making ourselves or some person or thing an idol. St. Paul, especially in his letter to the Romans, speaks of sin as acting apart from faith. Sin involves seeking hope where it cannot be found. It is searching for fulfillment in people or situations which seem life-giving, when in reality they bring only death.

It is possible to experience self-hate and guilt because of sin, to find sin where none exists, to think of everything as sinful. We can view God as an avenging judge and punisher. If we look at sin like that, we will be miserable because we have not taken into account the Gospel's message. Of course, it is also possible to deny sin completely and live as though sin does not exist. We need to recognize the existence of sin, at the same time recognizing the incredible love and forgiveness of God.

As we read Scripture, it is very clear that Jesus constantly practiced forgiveness and that he associated with recognized sinners. His friends included Mary Magdalene, Zacchaeus and Matthew who were hated tax collectors, and Peter who denied him. The images Jesus used to describe his Father were far from that of an avenging judge. He presented his Father as a king who is merciful, as a woman looking for a lost coin, as a collector canceling a large debt, as a shepherd looking for lost sheep, as a Jewish father running to embrace his sinful son. God is always ready to forgive. As theologian Hans Küng puts it, Jesus made some people angry because he went about "dumping mercy indiscriminately on all people."

For Reflection on Part I

1. According to John Shea, "sin is forgetfulness of creaturehood." Can you think of some concrete examples that would illustrate this definition?

_____

_____

_____

2. Can you describe some concrete situations in which St. Paul's description of sin might be applied?

_____

_____

_____

3. Think of as many examples as possible from Jesus' life when he forgave sin and accepted sinners. If you were asked to describe Jesus as a forgiving person, how would you do it?

_____

_____

_____

4. Someone has described sin as doing anything that hurts you or someone else. What are the strengths of such a definition? What are the weaknesses?

_____

_____

_____

Part II—Sin and Forgiveness in the Gospel

Let us look at one Gospel story that reveals much about sin and forgiveness. It is the story of the woman at Simon's supper recorded in Luke 7:36–50.

"One of the Pharisees invited Jesus to a meal. When he arrived at the Pharisee's house and took his place at table, a woman came in, who had a bad name in the town. She had heard he was dining with the Pharisee and had brought with her an alabaster jar of ointment. She waited behind him at his feet, weeping, and her tears fell on his feet, and she wiped them away with her hair; then she covered his feet with kisses and anointed them with the ointment.

"When the Pharisee who had invited him saw this, he said to himself, 'If this man were a prophet, he would know who this woman is that is touching him and what a bad name she has.' Then Jesus took him up and said, 'Simon, I have something to say to you.' 'Speak, Master,' was the reply. 'There was once a creditor who had two men in his debt; one owed him five hundred denarii, the other fifty. They were unable to pay, so he pardoned them both. Which of them will love him more?' 'The one who was pardoned more, I suppose,' answered Simon. Jesus said, 'You are right.'

"Then he turned to the woman. 'Simon,' he said, 'you see this woman? I came into your house, and you poured no water over my feet, but she has poured out her tears over my feet and wiped them away with her hair. You gave me no kiss, but she has been covering my feet with kisses ever since I came in. You did not anoint my head with oil, but she has anointed my feet with ointment. For this reason I tell you that her sins, her many sins, must have been forgiven her, or she would not have shown such great love. It is the man who is forgiven little who shows little love.' Then he said to her, 'Your sins are forgiven.' Those who were with him at table began to say to themselves, 'Who is this man, that he even forgives sins?' But he said to the woman, 'Your faith has saved you; go in peace.' "

Let us consider what this woman had experienced. She was evidently aware of her sinfulness through her contact with the love and care of Jesus. She was a public sinner. When she realized what she was doing with her life, she *could* have become guilty or self-hating. Guilt and self-hate would have turned her inward. A real awareness of ourselves as sinners and of God as a loving God moves us to reach out for help. The woman in the Gospel was able to say, "I am selfish; I use people; I sell my body; I am deceitful"; but she was not destroyed in admitting this. Her self-knowledge was a grace that moved her to receive the forgiveness Jesus was ready to give. Jesus was then and is now eager to forgive seventy-times-seven times and more.

When we are guilty of sin and are willing to be forgiven, we experience new life, new growth. Forgiveness is an experience in which the sinner (the woman) and the person forgiving (Jesus) both participate. The good that Jesus called forth in the woman brought her to a new sense of her own worth. His loving forgiveness brought her to a new appreciation, to a new level of gratitude, to a new depth of love. Since much was forgiven her, she loved much. It was at this point of deep gratitude for forgiveness and new life that we find the woman at this supper. It is very possible that she simply wanted to symbolize her gratitude by anointing the feet of Jesus with myrrh, but she remembered clearly her sin and his forgiveness. That brought to the surface all the deep feelings connected with her experience, and she wept—unable to hold back her authentic expression of love and thanksgiving. Jesus' response to her was magnificent. Though the situation must have been somewhat awkward, he received and affirmed her action, appreciated her gesture and held her up as an example to his Pharisee host. Then, because we are healed gradually of sinfulness, Jesus said to her, "Your sins are forgiven." Finally, he commended her and sent her back encouraged to continue her new life, "Your faith has saved you; go in peace."

Look at our own stories; look at the story of the world. They are not so different; we are all sinners. It is a special moment when any one of us recognizes sin, calls it by name, and asks for forgiveness and healing. This is a grace. True self-worth and the ability to reconcile ourselves with others—to be a healing people in a world in need of healing—is found in the experience of God's acceptance and forgiveness. We need to recognize what is good, healthy, and whole in us and around us, and to see it as a sign of what we can become. We also need to appraise our value systems, our relationships, our life-styles, and our national structures and to be dissatisfied with all that dehumanizes. It is in these places that we need to avail ourselves of the healing and forgiving power of God who loves us unconditionally and accepts us totally.

For Reflection on Part II

1. You have experienced your own sinfulness in a very real way at some time in your life. Describe that situation and your feelings.

_____

_____ _____

2. You have been hurt deeply by another person at some time in your life. Describe that experience.

_____

_____

Do you feel that that hurt is healed, or does it still need healing?

_____

_____

3. You have been healed in some way and have experienced God's love and forgiveness. Describe one of these times and your feelings about that experience.

_____

_____

4. You are aware of social sin in the world (racism, sexism, starvation, exploitation of developing countries, etc.). Has one evil of society touched you personally? Have you been involved in any way in alleviating social evils? Describe the involvement.

_____

_____

Healing and Hallowing

In his *New Catholic World* article "Catechetics in a Future Tense," John Nelson makes a point applicable to our discussion on sin and forgiveness. He says: "The present thrust . . . moves in two complementary directions, healing and hallowing. The healing is prophetic. It calls people to appraise realistically the value-systems by which we live, to recognize where we dehumanize one another, and to exorcise this demon from among us. It provokes indignation, a dissatisfaction with things as they are so that we may make them better. Equally important is the hallowing. It recognizes the good and the healthy already with us, not as a final goal, but as a sign of what people can become. If the healing exorcises, the hallowing divinizes."

Prayer above all should aim to allow these two complementary directions, healing and hallowing, to work in our lives. To recognize and be dissatisfied with things as they are is a part of prayer: "Thy kingdom come; thy will be done on earth as it is in heaven. . . . And forgive us our trespasses."

As we read the Gospels, we see that Jesus related to many people. He healed and hallowed ("blessed") over and over again. For us, just as for Jesus, a life of prayer will result in healing and hallowing. We should not think of healing, however, only in physical terms. Healing is also emotional, psychological, and spiritual. Jesus forgave sins, blessed the little children, and brought calm in anxious moments. He will do the same for us. To be touched by this twofold movement of healing and hallowing, we sinners must enter into a relationship with Jesus Christ, even, and especially, in our sinfulness.

In our sinfulness, we are like the rough-hewn chunks of ore of a precious metal, which must be washed and processed and melted down in fire before they can be polished. Bringing out the hidden brilliance of the metal is a long, arduous process. We must remember this in regard to our sinful selves. To become better—"perfect, as our heavenly Father is perfect"—takes a prayerful attitude, consciousness about ourselves and an acceptance of God's forgiveness and redeeming love, which alone brings about healing. John Henry Newman once said, "To live is to change; to be perfect is to have changed often."

The other side of the coin, or hallowing, is recognizing the good and healthy already in us, not as the final goal, but as a sign or pledge of what we can become. St. Paul put it beautifully when he wrote: "Be like children of light, for the effects of the light are seen in complete goodness and light living and truth" (Ephesians 5:9). We should radiate the joy and gratitude of a child, who does not see a hill as an obstacle, but as a challenge and opportunity to climb and slide and roll down. It is that kind of prayerful gratitude and joy that will truly hallow our lives from day to day.

So often we approach the realities of sin and forgiveness in our lives in a negative way. People who pray from a realization of their sinfulness and need for forgiveness, however, do so out of a keen sense of the healing and hallowing touch of God upon their lives. Psychiatrists are quick to point out that there is no such thing as a nervous breakdown; the nerves do not break down from stress—*we* break down from fear, *undue fear.* Prayer can free us from fear by allowing us to participate in a loving relationship with God that will enable us to realistically appraise ourselves—our gifts and goodness, our sins, and our need for forgiveness. With this prayerful attitude, even in our sinfulness we should be able to stand before the Lord, relaxed and without fear.

The Jews have a beautiful word that Jesus would have known and used: *Shalom.* It is a greeting and farewell and means wholeness, peace-harmony, healing-hallowing, integrity. *Shalom* is never an accomplished fact; rather it indicates something to be found, discovered or experienced. It involves the restlessness of search, an honest and prayerful search for the healing-hallowing elements of our lives. Reconciliation is to live in the spirit of *Shalom!*

For Reflection

Do you know anyone who is a recovered alcoholic or drug addict? If you do, and that person has done the "Twelve Steps of Alcoholics Anonymous," ask for an explanation of the fourth and fifth steps. Or call your local chapter of Alcoholics Anonymous, Al-Anon, or Narcotics Anonymous and ask them for some literature on the fourth and fifth steps.

When you have thoughtfully read and understood the steps, reflect on them. Then write in your journal, and pray over your own kind of personal fourth and fifth steps.

The Lord's Prayer

In his book *Bread for the Wilderness, Wine for the Journey,* John Killinger writes about a young man who was distressed about a medical problem. In his mental anguish and apprehension, he thought it might be more relevant to pray the Lord's Prayer as follows:

> Our Father, who art in heaven
> why aren't you down here on earth,
> doing something about my present difficulty?
> Who cares if your name is hallowed,
> or whether or not your kingdom comes,
> when what concerns us most
> is what life is really made of—
> our big and little hurts. . . .

But, instead, this is what he wrote:

> Our Father, in spite of the present difficulty, you are still in heaven and the world is still ordered. May my response hallow your name. The coming of your kingdom is more important than my own difficulty—so may I not hinder its coming by my worry.
> Cause this event to be an opening up to
> > your will for earth
> > which I cannot see as clearly
> > as if I were in heaven.
> I must recognize that you still provide
> > the necessities of life:
> > I have bread enough.
> May this event help me to realize how important it is
> > to secure your forgiveness
> > and to forgive those who have sinned against me.
> And may this not be an occasion for temptation
> > to lose faith or respond as a pagan.
> Deliver me from any evil response or action in this difficulty.
> The overriding and all-important fact of life
> > is that to you belongs the kingdom,
> > and the power and the glory forever,
> > and this event is caught up in that fact.
> > Amen.

For Reflection

1. In the first paraphrase of the Our Father, the writer questions God, is perturbed by him, wonders if he cares. Have you ever felt that way? Does it feel O.K. to you to have those feelings?

2. What feelings and insights are expressed in the second paraphrase of the Our Father? What makes this kind of prayer possible for the author or for ourselves?

3. Would you change or add any lines to what has been expressed if you were writing a personal version of the Our Father?

Scripture and Meditations on Forgiveness

Read the following Scripture passages. Use the questions to reflect on God's personal love and forgiveness.

1. Isaiah 40:1–5:

- How has God consoled his people?
- How has he consoled you?
- How have you consoled his people?
- How have you prepared yourself for God's love and forgiveness?

2. Luke 7:36–50:
- The woman has been forgiven; how does she respond?
- How does Jesus respond to her?
- How is sinfulness a "happy fault" for her? For you?

3. Luke 15:11–32:
- What are your feelings toward each character in the story?
- What does the story tell you about the father?
- What does the story tell you about forgiveness?

Bibliography

Books
Camara, Helder. *The Desert Is Fertile.* New York: Orbis Books, 1976.
Hellwig, Monika. *The Eucharist and the Hunger of the World.* New York: Paulist Press, 1976.
Kushner, Harold S. *When Bad Things Happen to Good People.* New York: Schocken Books, 1981.
Leach, George. *Hope for Healing.* New York: Paulist Press, 1978.
Linn, Dennis and Matthew Linn. *Healing of Memories.* New York: Paulist Press, 1978.
———. *Healing Life's Hurts.* New York: Paulist Press, 1978.
MacNutt, Francis. *The Prayer That Heals.* Notre Dame: Ave Maria Press, 1981.
Nouwen, Henri. *The Living Reminder.* New York: Seabury Press, 1977.
Sanford, John A. *Evil.* New York: Crossroad Press, 1981.
Shea, John. *The Challenge of Jesus.* Chicago: Thomas More Press, 1975.
Sheed, Francis J. *Our Hearts Are Restless.* New York: Seabury Press, 1976.
———. *The Lord's Prayer.* New York: Seabury Press, 1975.
Vanier, Jean. *Be Not Afraid.* New York: Paulist Press, 1975.
———. *Community of Growth.* New York: Paulist Press, 1979.

Articles
Hug, James E. "Call to Cultural Conversion," *New Catholic World,* Paulist Press, New York, July/August 1983.
Nelson, John. "Catechetics in a Future Tense," *New Catholic World,* Paulist Press, New York, Jan./Feb. 1972.

Record
"We Will Build the City of God," *The Lord of Light.* St. Louis Jesuits. Phoenix, Arizona: North American Liturgy Resources, 1981.

Chapter 10

Interplay of Stories

Interplay of Stories

Part I—God's Story and Ours

Prayer leads us to see that God's life is connected with our lives, that the story of God and the story of humankind are interrelated. The one great story, in fact, is the story of God bringing all of humankind back to himself.

St. John's Gospel ends with the sentence, "There were many other things that Jesus did; if all were written down, the world itself, I suppose, would not hold all the books that would have to be written." This exaggeration does not mean that the world could not hold all the books containing the facts of Jesus' life. The facts could fit in a large volume, but the implications, the effects, the changed lives, and the power and influence of his word and life would require more books than the world could hold. God's relationship with us and our response to him is an unfinished story; it is one story, and each of us is part of it. The birth of a baby, the death of a loved one, and the conversion of a friend are events that are a part of the great story of God bringing his people back to himself.

God so loved us that he came to live among us; he sent his Son Jesus as the Messiah. The faith journey of Jesus is a very significant part of God's life among us. His journey is a source of our faith and our hope and a source of leadership for us. So much of Jesus' work and message was given in the context of ordinary, daily events. We tend to view many of the daily events of our lives as "necessary, but not very important." One way to become more spiritually aware is to begin recognizing the value of each daily, ordinary event and God's presence in it.

Consider the significant encounters that Jesus had with individuals in very ordinary situations. Take the story of the Samaritan woman (John 4:7–26). After Jesus introduced himself and began to talk with the woman, the conversation moved from a simple request by Jesus for a drink of water to a declaration by the woman that he was the Messiah. Imagine moving from a request for water to faith during a short conversation! Obviously the woman was receptive; she spent time with Jesus, she let herself be known, she let herself be touched by his word.

His word was a promise to quench thirst. "Whoever drinks this water will get thirsty again; but anyone who drinks the water that I shall give will never be thirsty again: the water that I shall give will turn into a spring inside him, welling up to eternal life" (John 4:14). The life he speaks of, once consciously received, springs up, grows and overflows into life everlasting. The woman received the word of life from Jesus and she simply could not keep that life, that good news, to herself. She went into the town and told all the people she met about the deep quality of life she found in this man who forgave and healed and and strengthened her.

For Reflection

1. Use your imagination and try to think of the many people who have been affected by Jesus' life. Look back in Jesus' history and recall names of people. Look into your own personal history. Can you name people you know who are conscious of being affected by Jesus' life?

2. Consider the value of recognizing the presence of God in your daily life. How does it make you feel when you become conscious of God's presence? Describe this experience.

3. Have you ever gotten to know someone really well during some seemingly accidental meeting? Jesus made a difference in the life of the woman at the well simply because he needed a drink of water. He took advantage of this everyday life situation to touch someone's life. Has there ever been a time in your life when you were able to touch another through a casual meeting? As you reflect on the occasion, are you aware of the presence of God in that meeting?

Part II—Living Ordinary Life

On another occasion Jesus was speaking to a crowd. The people became hungry. Jesus, sensitive to their needs, inquired if there was enough food for them. This was the occasion when he miraculously multiplied the loaves and the fishes. After all had eaten, Jesus spoke his word of life. "I am the bread of life. He who comes to me will never be hungry; he who believes in me will never be thirsty. . . . I am the living bread which has come down from heaven. Anyone who eats this bread will live forever; and the bread that I shall give is my flesh, for the life of the world" (John 6:35. 51). Many did not understand, but some accepted Jesus' word.

The two stories we have just considered took place under circumstances that are familiar to us. Asking for a drink of water from a friend and then listening with our hearts to her story of feeding a hungry husband and children is something we might do in everyday life. Our listening indicates our interest, care and love. As was the case with Jesus and the Samaritan woman, we do more than have a drink of water; we give the life and strength of love. Jesus spent his energy in activities that created a quality of life: loving, hoping, suffering, being present, turning the other cheek, and even laying down his life for his friends. We need to become more and more conscious of the connections between our lives and the life of Jesus. Like him, we need to spend our days giving life, and we need to see that spending as a holy activity—a part of the one great story of God and humankind working together.

We are not alone. Our suffering is connected with the suffering of Jesus—his being misunderstood, rejected, arrested and ultimately crucified. His suffering is connected to the suffering of victims of racism in South Africa, of bloodshed in Ireland and the Middle East, of religious persecution in South America, and to the agony of starving millions, the pain of the handicapped and the retarded, and the sorrows of all those needing healing throughout the world. We are those who are suffering, those who are inflicting suffering and those who are relieving suffering. St. Paul referred to our suffering and his own as making up what is lacking in the suffering of Christ. What he was referring to was making a connection between the suffering of Christ and our own suffering and the suffering of all humankind. And so, one great story goes on and will go on until the end of time. Our personal stories are pages in the book of life too large for the world to hold. Our awareness of the connections between the story revealed in Scripture and our own stories grows as we reflect together on both stories.

Interconnections
Jesus, My Life and Our World

In the spaces provided, write brief descriptions of the experiences of Jesus, yourself and our world in regard to each topic. Reflect on the connections between these stories.

	Jesus' Life	My Life	Our World
Suffering			
Healing			
Feeding			
Celebrating			

Connections:
My Life and the Life of Jesus

Directions: Reflect on each of the activities named and on the examples suggested. Add a personal example to those included. How would you forgive, thank, etc.? What would your feelings, thoughts, and words be?

Jesus' Life	My Life

FORGIVING

- of Peter who denied him
- of the good thief

- of a friend who betrayed a confidence
- of a daughter or son who defied you

_____
_____
_____
_____
_____
_____
_____
_____

THANKING

- by gifting us with the Eucharist
- by sharing loaves and fishes with the crowd who listened to him

- by hugging a child
- by making a phone call

_____
_____
_____
_____
_____
_____

LISTENING

- to the needs of lepers
- to the needs of the Samaritan woman
- to the apostles in the storm

- to a person in a nursing home
- to a friend whose husband or wife has left

_____
_____
_____

Jesus' Life	My Life

HEALING

- of the paralytic
- of the woman with the hemorrhage
- of the little girl raised to life
- of the sinful woman at Simon's supper

- being with a person whose loved one has died
- embracing a friend whose spouse had a heart attack

_____

_____

_____

_____

WAITING

- for the apostles to understand
- for the rich young man to be ready to give all
- for an understanding of his own mission

- for a child to be born
- for a fifteen-year-old son to talk to you again

_____

_____

_____

_____

CELEBRATING

- at the feast of Cana
- at dinner with Zacchaeus
- at breakfast on Lake Tiberias after the resurrection

- at Christmas time
- at a birthday party
- at an anniversary dinner
- at a Thanksgiving liturgy

_____

_____

_____

_____

LOVING

- in his relationship with Mary Magdalene
- in a time of weeping over Lazarus
- in laying down his life for us

- in commitment to a spouse
- in care of an aged parent
- in concern for the hungry of the world

_____

_____

_____

_____

Waiting for Insight

One cannot learn to pray simply by reading this book. It is necessary to stop, to become quiet, to become attuned to one's feelings, and to listen to one's heart. Then the reflection in silence, the waiting, will provide "interconnections," or "insights." The following excerpts are from an article by John S. Dunne in *Prayer, Ritual and the Spiritual Life*. He provides some significant insights on "interconnections."

I would like to reflect on the experience of waiting on God. It is, I believe, the heart of prayer. It is a waiting on a God who is hidden in the darkness, not only the darkness that comes before and after life, but also the darkness that is found again and again during life whenever one is searching for one's way. The waiting is the praying, and the coming of God is the answer to the prayer, and His coming takes the form of a kindling of light in the darkness. This kindling of light I shall call "insight."

*　　*　　*

Imagine a man who has come to a time of darkness in his life when he doesn't know which way to go. . . . Ordinarily a person would go through two stages in reaching a decision. First he would explore the possibilities in his mind, imagining himself into them . . . then at length he would make his choice. . . . The first stage by itself does not ordinarily lead to a resolution. It only reveals the possibilities and their consequences. . . . Let us imagine a man who halts between the exploration of possibilities and the choice and waits for insight. . . . When he was exploring the possibilities, he was calculating advantages and disadvantages. . . . Now as he waits for insight, he is not looking for an error in his calculations or for a new balance of advantages. He is looking rather for a new vision of the way. When he was calculating, he was working out of the question, "What shall I do with my life?" Now, as he waits for insight, he is asking a different question, "Is there something my life wants to do with me?" or, if he is confident that his life does have a goal of its own, independent of any purpose he tries to impose upon it, then, "What does my life want of me?"

*　　*　　*

His first question comes first, "Is there something my life demands of me or calls upon me to do?" He fears that anything he may find in his life will turn out to be something he has put there himself. . . . A good sign that it is a true call, he reasons, would be if it went against his wishes. . . . On further thought it occurs to him that there could be a part of him that does not want the call and another part of him that does. . . . A call that goes against one wish could be in accord with another. . . . So the fact that a call is against certain of his wishes, he is forced to conclude, is no sign that it is a true call. Indeed maybe a call is always in accord with one's deepest wishes. . . . Maybe the call is the heart's desire and one is led by one's heart.

*　　*　　*

BEHOLD, THERE WILL APPEAR THE LORD
AND HE WILL NOT DECEIVE:
IF HE SHOULD DELAY, KEEP ON WAITING FOR HIM,
BECAUSE HE WILL SURELY COME AND WILL NOT TARRY.

*　　*　　*

If that is true, then in waiting for insight, he sees, he is waiting for his heart to speak. What he should be doing while he is waiting is listening to the different voices within himself? . . . Now he is entering into the second question, "What does my life demand of me?" The first question, nevertheless, is still in the back of his mind and comes to the fore whenever the inner voices seem to conflict. . . . Kierkegaard's saying comes to mind, "Purity of heart is to will one thing." The man we are imagining is searching his heart for that one thing. . . . He searches and searches, but does not find it. . . . For a moment he thinks he has fallen back into calculative thinking, for those inner voices are urging the very same things he was considering when he was calculating his possible courses of action. Yet he realizes now that he is no longer calculating but listening . . . listening to the sources of these calculations. He is trying to find out what part of himself is speaking when he hears a given voice and its promptings. . . . The only thing that is over and above all these voices is his own listening. That, he reflects, may be the unifying factor, his listening, his waiting for insight. In fact, the waiting, he begins to see, is the willing of one thing. He is willing one thing insofar as he is waiting for one thing, the unknown path he must walk. . . . Yet he is still in darkness. . . . He begins to worry about the amount of time he is spending . . . fearing that he is simply being indecisive. . . . Still he continues to wait, seeing that the waiting itself is unifying everything in him and giving him purity of heart.

*　　*　　*

His own waiting for insight is a gathering of all his forces, a coming together of everything within him. If God leads by the heart, then God's leading should come to light, as it seems to be doing, when the heart becomes pure, when the heart begins to will one thing.

*　　*　　*

He is able now to pose the question of choice in terms of the heart. He has waited long enough for risks and calculations to recede into the background and for the question of the heart to come to the foreground. "Would my heart be in this?" he now asks of each possibility. . . . This question is so simple that it seems he could have asked it at any time. Still the waiting on insight has been a purification of his heart that has enabled him to pass from his initial fears and calculation of risks to the matter of his heart's desire. The question of the heart could have been asked at any time but only now has it become uppermost in his mind. It casts a light upon his alternatives . . . making it seem possible now to make a choice that is not arbitrary. Where before it seemed that he could go various ways, now it seems fairly clear that there is only one way.

*　　*　　*

He makes his choice. As he makes it though, he is aware that he is not entirely sure of himself. . . He makes his decision with the awareness that he may be entirely wrong. In coming to his decision, however, he has not been seeking certainty so much as understanding and insight. . . . If his heart is not pure, if the path he has chosen is not that of heart's desire, if it is not the will of God for him, then he has hope that this will come to light as he travels the path. His waiting for insight continues on into the carrying out of his decision. He meets his uncertainty not by seeking for certainty—a quest that tends to defeat itself—but by continuing to wait for insight. His whole life becomes a waiting for insight and his hope is that he will be led from one insight to another, that his life will become a voyage of discovery. If he were to formulate as a prayer in words waiting for insight, it might go something like this: God! Where are You? I am lost. Show me the Way. . . . Yet prayer, as we have been speaking of it, could very well take the form of silence, a silence between the inner noise of calculative thinking and the outer noise of carrying out decision, a silent waiting in the darkness for the light to be kindled.

For Reflection

1. What insights or moments of "kindling light" have you experienced in your thought and prayer either alone or within a prayer group—insights about yourself, about God, about fellow human beings, about the world?
2. Do you have some awareness of your "heart's desire"? Are you closer to a response to Fr. Dunne's question, "What does my life want of me?"
3. Can you recall moments of waiting, of silence, of darkness that were painful, dull, challenging? Remember moments during this course or others that stand out as you look back on your life.

Bibliography

Baum, Gregory. *Journeys.* New York: Paulist Press, 1975.
Berthier, Rene *et al. Prayers for Everyday Life.* Notre Dame: Fides, 1974.
Callahan, Sydney and Ray Ellis. *The Magnificat.* New York: Seabury Press, 1975.
Callahan, William, S.J. *Noisy Contemplation.* Hyattsville, Md.: Quixote Center, 1982.
Carroll, James. *The Winter Name of God.* New York: Sheed and Ward, 1975.
Coughlin, Kevin. *Finding God in Everyday Life.* New York: Paulist Press, 1981.
Frank, Anne. *The Diary of a Young Girl.* New York: Modern Library, 1952.
Griffin, Robert. *I Never Said I Didn't Love You.* New York: Paulist Press, 1977.
————. *In the Kingdom of the Lonely God.* New York: Paulist Press, 1973.
Haring, Bernard. *Prayer: The Integration of Faith and Life.* Notre Dame: Fides, 1975.
Haring, Bernard and Ray Ellis. *Blessed Are the Pure of Heart.* New York: Seabury Press, 1977.
Houselander, Frances Carryll. *The Reed of God.* New York: Sheed and Ward, 1944.
Keller, Helen A. *The Story of My Life.* New York: Doubleday, 1952.
Novak, Michael. *Ascent of Mountain, Flight of Dove.* New York: Harper and Row, 1971.
O'Connor, Elizabeth. *The New Community.* New York: Harper and Row, 1976.
O'Meara, Thomas, O.P. *Loose in the World.* New York: Paulist Press, 1974.
Palmer, Parker J. *The Promise of Paradox.* Notre Dame: Ave Maria Press, 1980.
Shea, John. *Stories of God.* Chicago: Thomas More Press, 1978.
Stuhlmueller, Carroll, C.P. *Thirsting for the Lord.* New York: Alba House, 1977.
Tully, Mary Jo. *A Family Book of Praise.* New York: Sadlier, 1980.
Van Kaam, Adrian. *Looking for Jesus.* Denville: Dimension Books, 1977.
Westley, Richard. *Redemptive Intimacy.* Mystic: Twenty-Third Publications, 1981.